REINCARNATION — A BIBLICAL DOCTRINE ?

WHOSE TIME HAS COME FOR THE EVANGELICAL CHRISTIAN

by

MARILYNN McDIRMIT, D.D.

DOCTRINE — "That which is held to be true by any person, sect, or school, especially in religion."
Britannica World Language Dictionary

Dear Reader,

For many who pick up this book to read & hopefully study, a difficult decision was made. It _may_ seem to contradict what you have been taught. I sympathize with you completely, for I went through the same growth decision.

May I ask that you prayerfully meditate, asking only the Holy Spirit to guide & direct. He is waiting & eager to do just that!

I am praying for you.

Sincerely,

Marilynn McDirmit

EAGLE PUBLICATION CO.
P.O. Box 159
Maggie Valley, NC 28751

ISBN 0-9623953-1-5

TABLE OF CONTENTS

This book has been written

under the inspiration of GOD

through the love of JESUS CHRIST

guided by the perfect teacher, the HOLY SPIRIT

"And I, brethren, when I came to you, came not with excellency of speech or of wisdom, declaring unto you the testimony of God."

I Corinthians 2:1 (*KJV*)

"When I came to you, my brothers, to preach God's secret truth, I did not use big words and great learning."

I Corinthians 2:1 (*Good News Bible*)

DEDICATION

I humbly dedicate this book to those many Bible believing Christians who sincerely love the Bible, but realize that many questions are not answered in the 66 Books of the Old and New Testament . . . or have they just listened to what they have been told . . . or casually read?

With **only** the Holy Spirit as our teacher, let us study the Bible with a completely open and receptive mind and heart.

To my husband, Evan, for his patience, proofreading, help with research, and support in every possible way.

To the Rev. Dr. Roberta S. Herzog, a Christian Jewess, who taught me to study **all** Truth on **many** different levels.

"To every thing there is a season, and a time to every purpose under the heaven . . . a time to keep silence, and a time to speak."

Ecclesiastes 3:1,7b

PART I

REINCARNATION — A BIBLICAL DOCTRINE?

WHOSE TIME HAS COME FOR THE EVANGELICAL CHRISTIAN.

PREFACE

EVANGELICAL / FUNDAMENTAL / ORTHODOX / BORN-AGAIN CHRISTIANITY all denote a Christian that believes basically *only* the 66 books of the New and Old Testaments comprising THE HOLY BIBLE as the *only* foundation upon which any teaching or doctrine can be based since *"All scripture is given by inspiration of God, and is profitable for doctrine, for reproof, for correction, for instruction in righteousness"* (II Timothy 3:16).

And, *"Every word of God is pure; he is a shield unto them that put their trust in him. Add thou not unto his words, lest he reprove thee, and thou be found a liar."* (Proverbs 30:5,6) also believing *"For I testify unto every man that heareth the words of the prophecy of this book: If any man shall add unto these things, God shall add unto him the plagues that are written in this book: And if any man shall take away from the words of the book of this prophecy, God shall take away his part out of the book of life, and out of the holy city, and from the things which are written in this book."* (Revelation 22:18,19)

Therefore they accept and receive only those teachings and/or doctrines that can be found or proven in the 66 books of the Holy Bible.

It is for this reason that this PART I is based on that ONE book, THE HOLY BIBLE, King James Version, due to the worldwide acceptance of that particular translation of the scriptures.

The term Evangelical Christian will be used meaning a Fundamental, Orthodox, Born-Again, Biblical Christian since the terms are somewhat synonymous.

In Bible Numerology, the number two (2) is the number of witnessess and any doctrine or teaching must have at least two scripture passages to be considered valid.

That requirement will be satisfied . . . for as the Evangelical would say, "The Bible is its own best commentary."

Any special emphasis *in the scripture references themselves* is done by the author for special noting.

INTRODUCTION

Part of what makes the Bible so unique is that it has been written on at least three different levels of understanding — clearly indicated as: 1. the milk, 2. the meat, and 3. the strong meat of the Word.

"As newborn babes, (newborn babe — a soul who has just awakened or become aware of a desire, in this lifetime, to grow spiritually . . . that 'hungers and thirsts after righteousness' Matthew 5:6 . . . a soul that to the Evangelical, repents, is reborn, born-again, or converted) *desire the sincere milk of the word, that ye may grow thereby; If so be ye have tasted that the Lord is gracious."* (I Peter 2:2,3)

". . . For everyone that useth milk is unskilful in the word of righteousness; for he is a babe." (Hebrews 5:13)

It is believed that the 'milk' of scripture is the direct understandable meaning which can be learned at the first reading . . . taken directly from the immediate scripture since this is the easiest to understand or 'digest'.

Paul implies a responsibility of the teacher to develop the Christians from the 'milk' diet to the 'meat' diet, for he said he would not always feed them milk. They would and **should** have a desire to mature to the 'meat' level. (I Cor. 3:2)

Meat requires chewing (maturing) to digest. The soul is motivated as it has been said, *"How sweet are Thy words unto my taste! Yea, sweeter than honey to my mouth!"* (Psalms 119:103)

The charge to be weaned from a milk diet is given, *"Whom shall he teach knowledge? and whom shall he make to understand doctrine? them that are weaned from the milk, and drawn from the breasts."* (Isaiah 28:9)

"In the mean while his disciples prayed him, saying, Master, eat. But he saith unto them, "I have meat to eat that ye know not of." (John 4:31,32)

"Jesus saith unto them, My meat is to do the will of him that sent me, and to finish his work." (John 4:34) *"And did all eat the same spiritual meat."* (I Cor. 10:3)

Strong meat not only requires the putting together of scripture to understand the direct meaning, but also a real study and meditation is required to understand that which is NOT said.

Each would be encouraged, even admonished to seek the **strong meat**. *"For when for the time ye ought to be teachers, ye have need that one teach you again which be the first principles of the oracles of God; and are become such as have need of milk, and not of strong meat. For every one that useth milk is unskilful in the word of righteousness: for he is a babe.*

"But ***strong*** *meat belongeth to them that are of full age, even those who by reason of use have their senses exercised to discern* ***both*** *good and evil."* (Hebrews 5:12-14)

This book is particularly directed to those Evangelicals who have matured to at least the meat level in their study of the Bible and/or their personal experience. . . . and **anyone** else who is sincerely searching for deeper knowledge and full understanding.

God Bless, Marilynn McDermit

1

THE TRUE TEACHER

"But the Comforter, which is the Holy Ghost, whom the Father will send in my name, **he** *shall teach you all things, and bring all things to your remembrance, whatsoever I have said unto you.*

(John 14:26)

"But the anointing which ye have received of him abideth in you, and ***ye need not that any man teach you;*** *but as the same anointing teacheth you of all things . . ."*

(I John 2:27)

For those who have completely opened their minds and hearts, allowing only the Holy Spirit to be their teacher, as only **He** should (disregarding church teaching, even Bible schools and seminary teachings) . . . asking for THE ONLY TRUE AND PERFECT TEACHER to enlighted them, they are astounded and amazed at the seemingly 'new' and undiscovered depths of teaching revealed.

"Howbeit when he, the Spirit of Truth, is come, he will guide you unto ***all*** *truth: for he shall not speak of himself; but whatsoever he shall hear, that shall he speak:* ***and he will show you things to come."*** (John 16:13)

The Holy Spirit is in essence the infinite 'breath of God'. *"And when he had said this, he breathed on them, and saith unto them, Receive ye the Holy Spirit."* (John 20:22)

The Holy Spirit is in the world today with great power and wisdom, ready to be poured upon all who look to the Holy Spirit for guidance. The mission of the Holy Spirit is to bring all men into communion with God; to guide men in order that they will not mistake the way into the Light. JUST ASK! *"If any of you lack wisdom, let him ask of God, that giveth to all men liberally, and upbraideth not; and it shall be given him."* (James 1:5)

The Holy Spirit is third in the Trinity, which in theology

is designated: Father, Son, and Holy Spirit. Therefore, He is to be considered a member of the God-head.

The Holy Spirit is the authority of the gospel of Jesus. He is the **only** authority that Jesus ever recognized, and whoever attempts to set forth His gospel from any other standpoint is in the letter and not the spirit. No man can know what Jesus' doctrine is except he receives it direct from the one and only custodian. It is not to come second-hand, but each one for himself must receive it from the Holy Spirit, which is sent by the Father in the name of the Son.

The Bible does not contain even one **complete** teaching on any particular subject, so we must take topic references from various parts to synthesize a composite opinion.

However, we must be careful not to **prooftext,** but keep in **context** - or do not use a verse or a **part of a verse** in the Bible to prove a point, but take the entire verse and its total content (verses before and after).

We shall try diligently to use that which is known, proven, and accepted about God and Jesus the Christ, comparing it with that which we do read in the Bible, as the Holy Spirit has spoken to Bible Scholars.

Undoubtedly one of the most beautiful, Christ-like doctrines in the Bible has, until very recently, been ignored by most Evangelical Bible Scholars, Biblical teachers, and Bible believing Christians. This is the Doctrine of Reincarnation.

One of the reasons given is that it is not taught in the Bible . . . yet Biblical evidence for reincarnation is surprisingly conclusive and intimated strongly, in spite of councils and translators to obliterate it for their own particular reasons.

First, we must have a definition of reincarnation, for certainly there are many levels of interpretation. This book will deal with the definition found in Brittanica World

Language Dictionary, "A rebirth of the soul in successive bodies"; that is, **human** bodies. Most reincarnationists do not believe in transmigration, which is the belief that we started out as a fish or a monkey or whatever, then evolved to a human. Those reincarnationists that have a **spiritual** foundation, not just a scientific one, reject transmigration.

Believing as the Bible teaches, that God created man *"in our image, and after our likeness: and let them have dominion over all the earth."* (Genesis 1:26) (Man being a general term for man or woman.) Therefore, humans evolve through reincarnation into other human bodies for the purpose of becoming one with the Father ... *"That they all may be one as thou, Father, are in me, and I in thee, that they also may be one in us: that the world may believe that thou has sent me. And the glory which thou gavest me I have given them; that they may be one, even as we are one."* (John 17:21, 22)

2

WHERE IS THE WORD IN THE WORD? (BIBLE)

"To every thing there is a season, and a time to every purpose under the heaven . . . a time to keep silence, and a time to speak." (Ecclesiastes 3:1, 7b)

Fragments on reincarnation are scattered throughout the Bible. Direct statements and inferences prove it to be a definite teaching of the Bible, as beautiful, fair, just, and Christ-like as any teaching could be.

The Holy Spirit continues to reveal new truths from the Bible, as the 'season' for that truth becomes more perfect in God's timing, so let us have eyes to see and ears to hear the wonders He has prepared for us.

Many will say the word 'reincarnation' is not mentioned in the Bible — true, it was one of the doctrines waiting for it's 'season' or 'time' to the Bible believing Christian.

. . . But neither is the word 'rapture' mentioned in the Bible; yet the Rapture, as interpreted from Thessalonians *"For the Lord Himself shall descend from heaven with a shout, with a voice of the archangel, and with the trump of God: and the dead in Christ shall rise first: then we which are alive and remain shall be caught up together with them in the clouds, to meet the Lord in the air: and so shall we ever be with the Lord. Wherefore comfort one another with these words."* (I Thessalonians 4:16-18) is an established doctrine in approximately 90% of all Evangelical faiths; accepted by all Bible Scholars, whether pre-tribulation, mid-tribulation, or post-tribulation. (Please see PART III for definitions.) . . . and it has just the **one** reference **directly** connected with it.

It is assumed to be alluded to in the passage, *"Then shall two be in the field; the one shall be taken, and the other left. Two women shall be grinding at the mill; the one shall be taken, and the other left. Watch therefore: for ye know not what hour your Lord doth come."* (Matthew 24:40-42)

Yet **preceeding** the above verses is the passage — *"Immediately after the tribulation of those days shall the sun be darkened, and the moon shall not give her light, and the stars shall fall from heaven, and the powers of the heavens shall be shaken: And then shall appear the sign of the Son of man in heaven: . . .* (Matthew 24:29,30a)

We do know that the Rapture is a somewhat recently accepted doctrine, recognized certainly within the last century, and has become known as the Doctrine of the Rapture.

Reincarnation is not new, and has been widely accepted by Eastern religions. Therefore, bearing in mind that Jesus and His family, temple priests, believers, and contemporaries were a part of that Eastern religious community, we can be confident it was very well known to Jesus, the Christ, THE SON OF GOD, omnipotent — all powerful; omniscient — all knowledge; and omnipresent — ever present.

Another word, widely accepted by the evangelical community, but not directly found in the Bible, is Millennium, meaning — a period of a thousand years. In theology, the period of a thousand years during which Christ will reign on earth; a period of great happiness, peace, prosperity, etc.[1] *". . . and they lived and reigned with Christ a thousand years."* (Revelation 20:4d)

A thousand years in the Bible (or elsewhere) is a millennium, but in the particular context of the word 'millennium' used by Bible Scholars, it is usually meant that time after Christ has returned to earth and is ruling and reigning 'with His saints' on the earth.

Many of the scripture passages for the 'second coming' (the time preceeding these 1000 years) are debatable as to whether they refer to the 'second coming' or to the 'rapture' which is to preceed the 'second coming' by approximately seven (7) years.

[1]*Webster's New World Dictionary Of The American Language*

These two words, "Rapture" and "Millennium" are two concepts that have little foundation in the Bible, yet are widely accepted being built upon a teaching from the Bible where that 'word' given to the teaching is not found in the Bible.

I believe that "Reincarnation" is also a Biblical doctrine. Yet the many excellent books that are available on this subject have not discussed this interrelationship as will be developed further in this book.

3

WHAT IS LIFE?

". . . I am come that they might have life, and that they might have it more abundantly."

(John 10:10b)

"For God so loved the world, that he gave his only begotten Son, that whosoever believeth in him should not perish, but have **everlasting** *life."*

(John 3:16)

Let us consider if life is eternal and the purpose of this life.

The Bible, especially the New Testament, abounds with verses and passages that refer to everlasting life or eternal life. Many of those very familiar passages can be quoted by most Sunday School children — such as John 3:16, 26; Romans 6:23; John 6:47; Galatians 6:8 to name a few.

Consider also *"Lift up your eyes, and look on the fields; for they are white already to harvest. And he that reapeth receiveth wages, and gathereth fruit unto life eternal."*

(John 4:35b-36a)

The interpretation of these verses is that the soul of the human being lives forever.

YES, LIFE IS ETERNAL!

Reincarnation helps us to realize that **LIFE IS PURPOSEFUL** — after we become of 'age', the choices we make every moment of our lives are really important. No one is a victim of 'fate' because we all have FREE WILL. The one supreme desire and purpose of our soul is to become reunited with God. We keep our identity through our soul, which records every thought, word, and deed — as per the Book of Life (Revelation 20:12). Each embodiment (incarnated soul) has a lesson, or series of lessons, to learn to assist the soul to acquire the 'fruit' (not fruits) of the Spirit, which are love, joy, peace, longsuffering (patience), gentleness, goodness, faith, meekness (humility), and temperance (self-control). (See Galatians 5:22, 23a) The ultimate aim of the soul is to be perfect, as Jesus said, *"That they all may be one; as thou, Father, art in me, and I in thee, that they also may be one in us: that the world may believe that thou has sent me. And the glory which thou gavest me I have given them; that they may be one, even as we are one: I in them, and thou in me, that they may be made perfect in one."* (John 17:21-23a)

LIFE HAS MEANING AND PURPOSE! Reincarnation teaches that each life has a plan or a lesson to be learned — sometimes more than one, but there is a purpose **always**.

Let's look at John 9:1-3, *"And as Jesus passed by, he saw a man which was blind from his birth. And his disciples asked him, saying, Master, who did sin, this man, or his parents, that he was born blind? Jesus answered, Neither hath* ***this*** *man sinned,* ***nor*** *his parents: but that the works of God should be made manifest in him."*

These verses have continually bothered many, because it just doesn't seem consistant with our understanding of a loving God and Father who would allow this baby to be born blind, grow into manhood; his parents to suffer with him as their precious son found many pleasures denied him (and them) — waiting for the moment when Jesus would heal him.

BUT when you consider this in the light of reincarnation, this man, and his parents, had a lesson to be learned (what these lessons were is known only to their souls and God) but at that point in their lives, the lesson had been learned, and the blind man was healed! Consider also that from that time, the man and his parents were of great blessing to God's work and plan to further the ministry of Jesus the Christ.

As the disciples alluded to reincarnation regarding this man and his parents (remember, he was **born blind**). Jesus did not **deny** their thoughts on the matter; in fact, Jesus' denial to speak against reincarnation, is almost as strong as His speaking for it, as we shall see in a couple of examples later in this book.

Life is an opportunity. Each life is a time to learn, to grow more and more like Christ, for we are loved by a patient, merciful God who gives us the **free will** to learn at our own pace again, again and again.

4

THEN THE DISCIPLES UNDERSTOOD!

". . . Then the disciples ***understood*** *that he spake unto them of John the Baptist."*

(Matthew 17:13)

One of the most outstanding passages in my mind regarding this beautiful teaching is the one concerning John the Baptist.

"For all the prophets and the law prophesied until John. And if you will receive it, this **is** *Elias, which was for to come. He that hath ears to hear, let him hear."* (Spoken by Jesus, Himself, in Matthew 11:13-15)

But there is more . . . please do read the entire chapter of Matthew 17, however, we are especially concerned with just a portion at this time.

"And as they came down from the mountain, Jesus charged them, saying, Tell the vision to no man, until the Son of man be risen again from the dead. And his disciples asked him, saying, Why then say the scribes that Elias must first come? And Jesus answered and said unto them, Elias truly shall first come, and restore all things. But I say unto you, that Elias is come already, and they knew him not, but have done unto him whatsoever they listed. Likewise shall also the Son of man suffer of them. Then the disciples ***understood*** *that he spake unto them of John the Baptist."* (Matthew 17:9-13, also see Mark 9:11-13)

Realizing that Jesus is the Christ, acclaimed by God Himself, *"This is my beloved Son, in whom I am well pleased; hear ye him."* (Matthew 17:5b, also see Matthew 3:17, Mark 1:11, Luke 3:22, Luke 9:35, II Peter 1:17); and acknowledging that He (Jesus) had all knowledge and wisdom, certainly He now knew His disciples were understanding that Elias/Elijah was incarnated as John the Baptist — would Jesus **allow** them to misunderstand?

These were the men close to Him, chosen by Him,

upon whom He was committing the task of continuing His work and teachings, to instruct others, to write of their knowledge and wisdom concerning their experiences with Him for this entire Piscean Age* and the beginning of the Aquarian Age*. (See Part III for definitions.)

Therefore, (remember, when you see a therefore, meditate for a moment, look back and see why it is 'there for') Jesus was giving His assent by His silence to what the disciples had understood.

A beautiful doctrine to be brought to light 'in its season'.

5

SOWING AND REAPING

"Be not deceived; God is not mocked: for whatsoever a man soweth, that shall he also reap." (Galatians 6:7)

Along with the contemplation of the above verse, let us consider the following:

"But this I say, He which soweth sparingly shall reap also sparingly; and he which soweth bountifully shall also reap bountifully." (II Corinthians 9:6) . . . and

"With good will doing service, as to the Lord, and not to men: Knowing that whatsoever good thing any man doeth, the same shall he receive of the Lord, whether he be bond or free."

(Ephesians 6:7, 8)

This is a positive, definite law of God!

At this time, let me introduce to a majority of the Evangelical community a new word . . . **'karma'** meaning "the effect of any act, religious or otherwise; the law of cause and effect regulating one's future life, inevitable retribution." *(Brittanica World Language Dictionary)*

Returning to the Bible verse *"whatsoever a man soweth, that shall he also reap"* can actually be expressed another way by putting God's law in one word, Karma.

I know this next point touches on a subject many Evangelicals have had to face when pastors, teachers, counselors, and friends are asked this question many times . . . "why was I fortunate and blessed with being born in a beautiful, free, democratic country; of loving, devoted parents who very early in life taught me right from wrong and the priorities of life through loving discipline; always having **something** to eat and wear, a comfortable home where God was glorified, Jesus Christ was recognized and revered?"

The author, for one, can remember a friend who lived just down the street who had a drunken father who beat her and her mother; many times they had little or nothing to eat for days, clothes so tattered and torn she was the butt of many jokes at school; rarely knew what it was to be warm and comfortable at home, abused in **every** way by her father . . . the list could go on and on.

Why, God, I remember questioning in my young mind.

As time went on and the world became smaller through television and satellite communications, the inequalities seem to become greater and greater — not only limited to our neighborhood, nor our city, nor our state, nor our country.

I sincerely hope my friend has learned and conquered her lesson(s) and that she is happily married to a loving husband who provides her with delicious food, lovely clothes, and a harmonious home.

Certainly you have many examples of your own, too numerous to specifically mention — individuals who have done unimaginable harm and hurt to others, (at least unimaginable to the average law-abiding, loving citizen and Christian) . . . yet due to plenty of money, fame or just knowing the right people have seemingly 'reaped' very well in spite of their horrendous deeds.

To me, the Biblical Book of Job is a unique example of reincarnation. Why would our all-powerful, all-knowing, ever-present God have any desire or need to prove Himself to Satan through a human man, Job. A man, of whom it was said in Job 1:1 was *"perfect and upright, and one that feared (revered) God, and eschewed (shunned) evil"* or the blind man who *"had not sinned."* (John 9:1-3)

What is God's justification to permit these events happening unless they are related to a previous life? Could reincarnation be an answer to these questions? Could souls, through their free will, incarnate at a particular time and place, with certain parents and circumstances to help them learn the lessons they would be working on in that particular lifetime?

6

LITERAL MANSIONS IN HEAVEN — WHY?

Let not your heart be troubled: ye believe in God, believe also in me. In my Father's house are many mansions: if it were not so, I would have told you. I go to prepare a place for you. And if I go and prepare a place for you, I will come again, and receive you unto myself; that where I am, there ye may be also."

(John 14:1-3)

The Evangelical Christian believes that after his physical death, his soul goes to Heaven and he receives a 'mansion' in which to live throughout eternity. (There are happenings between these two events but for the purpose of this point, we are moving on.)

After all, hasn't he (the Evangelical Christian) been sending material to Heaven to build his mansion as per *"Lay not up for yourselves treasures upon earth, where moth and dust doth corrupt, and where thieves break through and steal: But lay up for yourselves treasures in heaven, where neither moth nor rust doth corrupt, and where thieves do not break through nor steal: For where your treasure is, there will your heart be also."* (Matthew 6:19-21)

Taking this passage and especially the word 'mansion' literally, WHAT POSSIBLE USE COULD WE HAVE FOR A MANSION OF THAT SORT?

Knowing what the Bible teaches us about Heaven (in the Evangelical literal sense) — that we will have a glorified body as Jesus Christ did after His resurrection, having no need of food, water, raiment, sleep, etc.; no one in Heaven is going to be a servant, and there would be no need of a mansion (where moth and rust doth corrupt, and thieves do not break through and steal).

No need for transportation, for we have but to think where we wish to be and there we are: through doors, etc. . . . as Jesus did when in His glorified body.

Then too, suppose the many outstanding Christians that have really earned a huge, beautiful mansion such as we might imagine the disciples had, of course . . . and bringing it down to later times, such spiritual giants as Dwight L. Moody, Dr. Harry Ironside, Dr. C. I. Scofield, Martin Luther, John and Charles Wesley, Sister Teresa, and on and on, naming only a few.

Certainly they would not consider themselves worthy, but their works have proven outstanding by the Evangelical community as a whole. Countless other great Biblical scholars and teachers have given their entire lives, **many** in martydom.

These spiritual 'giants' will have a beautiful mansion on Palace Boulevard, in the middle of Heaven, of course.

Several streets over will be Park Avenue, very lovely and somewhat elaborate for those souls who were 'saved' but did nothing particularly outstanding — such as faithful, hardworking ministers, and/or missionaries who affected many lives; perhaps reared in a Christian home, went to Bible School and Seminary and had many Christian advantages.

Then you might come to Cottage Place, where those who had very few, if any, Christian advantages or experiences — perhaps even being 'saved' later in life, having the majority of their lives spent in not knowing or caring about God and His laws or principles . . . or even had committed a terrible crime such as rape, murder, etc., and were only aware of their need of being 'saved' after they were sent to spend much of their life in prison, doing many good things while there, living decent and honorable lives even after being released . . . or the soul that began to see the error of his ways later in life, became a born-again Christian and lived for the Lord the rest of his life as Sunday School teacher, usher, choir member, or what **every** congregation needs, a faithful church member, supporter, and prayer warrior.

This latter group would fill the large majority of Heaven and rightfully so.

A few more streets over — wa-a-a-a-y over — is Shanty Town. These are souls that just made it, like the malefactor on the cross, *"And he said unto Jesus, Lord, remember me when thou comest into thy kingdom. And Jesus said unto him, Verily I say unto thee, Today shalt thou be with me in paradise."* (Luke 23:42, 43)

In scripture it is said there will be no sorrow in Heaven as well as **any** of the 'negative' emotions. Yet it is difficult for me (and has been for many years) to feel that the thief on the cross would live throughout eternity in Shanty Town and not be **quite** disturbed that he had so misspent his life — not doing things that had pleased God. The Evangelical feels that throughout eternity they will be singing praises to our wonderful Lord, and delighting to sit at the feet of Jesus just enjoying His presence. Consider that many of these people while on earth could hardly tolerate sitting in Church, and did not enjoy the fellowship of other Christians. Then why do they expect to delight in this Godly communion when they get to Heaven?

We will not even dwell on the fact of the Shanty Town inhabitant having a certain amount of 'righteous envy or sorrow' regarding those who had been blessed with all the advantages easing their life and right to live on Palace Boulevard, Park Avenue, Cottage Place, or wherever . . . while the Shanty Town inhabitant (perhaps) had a cruel, abusive family life, and heard of God only in angry cursing.

Yes, a literal mansion is totally unnecessary and against all that Jesus teaches us regarding Heaven.

Therefore, it is believed in Metaphysics (meta — beyond, higher, pertaining to the deeper Truths of the Bible rather than just the physical, literal meaning)* that the treasures we are sending to God are the materials to

*taken from *Webster's New World Dictionary*

form our next body, (mansion for the Holy Spirit); to help decide our parents, circumstances, and conditions enabling us, in our next life, to learn our lessons more effectively and easily, bringing us closer to the perfection Jesus talked about and that God so much desires.

7

WHAT IS DEATH?

"I protest by your rejoicing which I have in Christ Jesus our Lord, I die daily."

(I Corinthians 15:31)

This chapter will treat death through the eyes of reincarnational belief (realizing that, yes, there are many, many beliefs among the reincarnationists) as contrasted against Evangelical beliefs (again with many shades of beliefs).

One of the most difficult verses to encounter and explain when an Evangelical considers reincarnation is *"It is appointed unto men once to die, but after this the judgment;"* (Hebrews 9:27) May I encourage you to read the entire chapters of Hebrews 9 and I Corinthians 15.

Is it possible that as a Bible student/scholar/teacher we have been 'prooftexting' instead of 'contexting'? (See Chapter 1).

In the light of the verse, following the one directly quoted above *"So Christ was once offered to bear the sins of many; and unto them that look for him shall he appear the second time without sin unto salvation."* (Hebrews 9:28) and also *"But now is Christ risen from the dead, and become the* ***firstfruits*** *of them that slept."* (I Corinthians 15:20)

It is seen that these passages (especially if you read the entire chapters as listed above) places a whole new interpretation on this well-known scripture since it really is making a statement about the completion of the work of Christ. Actually, understanding the entire ninth chapter of Hebrews is necessary for grasping the beautiful truth that Jesus Christ was the bridge, so to speak, between the Old Testament (mostly law) and the New Testament (Grace).

"Think not that I am come to destroy the law, or the prophets: I am not come to destroy, but to fulfill." (Matthew 5:17) Jesus

fulfilled the Law of Sacrifice by being God's own sacrifice on the cross, thereby fulfilling the Old Testament Law of Sacrifice.

But Jesus, the Christ, had another great mission to perform . . . that of ushering in a new age, *giving a new commandment* and bringing a new covenant as prophecied *"Behold, the days come, saith the Lord, that I will make a new covenant with the house of Israel, and with the house of Judah . . . for I will forgive their iniquity, and I will remember their sin no more."* (Jeremiah 31:31, 34b)

This subject is a tremendous one — not particularly connected with this book, but you can see where and why these particular verses have a depth of meaning that we have just begun to comprehend.

As to the verse at the beginning of this chapter, Paul stated that he dies daily. Of course this is not in a literal sense, yet our present body temple **does** die a little each day, but if we are continually and constantly seeking to be more like Jesus Christ, then we are dying daily to carnel lusts, physical indulgences, and mental negative thoughts and/or idols.

The physical body of man truly does die once, and after that we are judged — by ourselves when confronted by our own life and what we desired to accomplish in our quest to return to the Father as a perfect being. (Please note again Jesus' prayer in John 17.)

8

ARE WE ALL FAILURES?

"But if the Spirit of him that raised up Jesus from the dead dwell in you, he that raised up Christ from the dead shall also quicken your mortal bodies by His Spirit that dwelleth in you."

(Romans 8:11)

As a young Bible School student, then a seminary student and countless times since, it has troubled me that Jesus expected and asked so much of His followers. Hard as I tried or hoped to attain, it seemed an impossible task, especially since I saw practically none of my excellent Bible Scholars (some of them world-renown), or my Evangelical friends accomplishing and/or attaining these same high standards or deeds. I sincerely don't wish to sound judgmental, but I do believe from the circles in which I traveled, I would have heard if someone had raised a person from the dead.

Jesus did say, *"Verily, verily (hear, hear, listen closely) I say unto you, He that believeth on me, the works that I do* ***shall he do also; and greater works than these shall he do;*** *because I go to my Father."* (John 14:12)

How could this be? Jesus was God in the flesh, how could mere mortal man possibly forgive a person of their sins as recorded *"And he saith unto her, Thy sins are forgiven."*

(Luke 7:48)

or *". . .* ***all*** *they that had any sick with divers diseases brought them unto him; and he laid his hands on* ***every one of them, and healed them.****"* (Luke 4:40b) also *". . . he cried with a loud voice, Lazarus, come forth. And he that was dead came forth, bound hand and foot with graveclothes: and his face was bound about with a napkin. Jesus saith unto them, Loose him, and let him go."* (John 11:43, 44) There are numerous other instances recorded in the Bible.

We all know of many 'healers' in Jesus' name, and I

have been to many such people and services. I have yet to go to one where **everyone** who requested healing was healed. In contacting them a year or so later, I learned their condition before 'healing' had returned . . . not **all** of course. I certainly felt I had the faith, because I had seen it happen and **know** God through the Holy Spirit could do it, I **never** was instantly healed. The continued prayers of loved ones and friends was the large contributing factor in my healing . . . and an important lesson learned!

Please do not entertain, for one moment, the thought that I do not believe in God's perfect Divine healing for I believe **ALL** healing is of God, many times through doctors, spiritual people with the particular gift of healing, etc. I would be the most foolish human alive if I believed that way because my life in this incarnation represents a practically perfect example of God's Divine healing from my very birth throughout my entire life. Even though I and my outstanding Christian parents certainly had the faith necessary for instantaneous healing, it just didn't happen to **me** that way.

Again, **ALL** healing, of course, is **Divine** healing. Many doctors readily admit that they are just the instruments of healing knowledge, and we truly thank God for His gift of doctors and their tremendous knowledge . . . but the healing is of God who created these 'full of wonder' (wonderful) bodies.

As a child, I was continually challenged by some type of disease in one way or another. This gave me much to think about. With the very spiritual parents I had, and my own desire to please God, with the excellent Bible teaching which I was constantly exposed — why didn't God instantly heal me so that I might be a better testimony for Him and His power. But I was learning patience and letting God do it HIS way in **His** own perfect timing.

My healings came through the knowledge and wisdom of doctors, through the many prayers of friends and loved ones, coupled with my own determination to be healed to do God's work and serve Him. I truly believe my life has been spared many times that I might do His will . . . in **His** time!

Do not think this is in any way a criticism, because I still take every opportunity to attend healing services. I'll accept anyone's sincere prayer (and there are **many** sincere people who are practicing the nine gifts of the Spirit as recorded in I Corinthians 12:7-11, one of which is healing). I am just stating a fact of which **I** can personally vouch . . . and having been a pastor's and missionary's wife, opportunities have been granted me to see and to observe many examples.

Yes, these 'greater works' have been done at times by a **very** few, perhaps unknown to you and me, but these have been souls that have reincarnated many times and have returned with a strong desire to serve and help others. They have learned many lessons, are Christ-like, or well along the way.

Have you attained this — been able to do these things that Jesus requested and said we **would** do — in **your** present lifetime?

If this chapter has seemed quite personal to you — it is because I have known and experienced these things . . . and who can know better than one who has gone through it? I know me and my thoughts better than anyone else can possibly do so; and I cannot know others thoughts and experiences so well.

Who knows **you** best? Your spouse or yourself? This is a personal salvation and way of life. You have been given the power to personally be Christ-like — and not self-like. As the Apostle Paul stated in I Corinthians 15:31b *"I die daily* (to self)."

9

PERFECTION ATTAINED?

"Be ye therefore perfect, even as your Father which is in heaven is perfect." (Matthew 5:48)

What an assignment for one lifetime! Can any of you really feel you have attained perfection when you haven't yet conquered patience . . . or anger . . . or the biggie, **fear**?

What a blessed peace we can have when we realize that God only has asked that we work on one or a few of these challenges in one lifetime, then have another opportunity through reincarnation to try again, in different circumstances, to be Christ-like.

How comforting to know that *"Being confident of this very thing, that he which hath begun a good work in you will perform it* ***until*** *the day of Jesus Christ."* (Philippians 1:6) Our becoming Christ-like is a continuous process.

How could we be 'confident' if we felt this must be done in one lifetime? But 'until the day of Jesus Christ' gives us possible hope of accomplishing that which is God's desire as Jesus prayed *"I in them, and thou in me, that they may be made perfect in one; and that the world may know that thou has sent me, and hast loved them, as thou hast loved me."* (John 17:23)

God does not give up on any soul *"But, beloved, be not ignorant of this one thing, that one day is with the Lord as a thousand years, and a thousand years as one day. The Lord is not slack concerning his promise, as some men count slackness; but is longsuffering to us-ward, not willing that any should perish, but that all should come to repentence."*(II Peter 3:8, 9)

Repentence means to desire with the intention to amend or change one way of thinking or doing.

Could that also mean a thousand lifetimes?

That magnificent promise that God gave to Abraham concerning his (Abraham) being the father of mighty nations, *"(As it is written, I have made thee a father of many nations,) . . . Who against hope believed in hope, that he might become the father of many nations, according to that which was spoken, . . . And being not weak in faith, he considered not his own body now dead, when he was about an hundred years old, neither yet the deadness of Sarah's womb: He staggered not at the promise of God through unbelief; but was strong in faith, giving glory to God; And being fully persuaded that, what he had promised, he was able also to perform."*(Romans 4:17-21)

Certainly God's promise to Abraham was not accomplished in one lifetime . . . but continues through thousands of years . . .

Probably many of you are asking "Why is there so **much** that is negative (sin), unhappiness of all kinds at this particular time when mankind has seemingly progressed so far?"

Many, many advanced souls are given the advantage of dealing with these negative experiences for their growth — just as other less evolved souls are dealing with the emotions, feelings, and problems that **they** need for their growth.

"But if the Spirit of him that raised up Jesus from the dead dwell in you, he that raised up Christ from the dead shall also quicken your mortal bodies by His Spirit that dwelleth in you."

(Romans 8:11)

What a loving and patient God we have!

10

FAITH OR WORKS?

"Even so faith, if it hath not works, is dead, being alone. Yea, a man may say, Thou hast faith, and I have works: shew me thy faith without thy works, and I will shew thee my faith by my works."

(James 2:17, 18)

Many Evangelicals are now probably saying, "But reincarnation seems to say that **I,** as an individual, am responsible, that it is works, not faith in Jesus, or grace."

Let us reason together. Faith and grace are so very important. Most Evangelicals believe that they must 'repent' and/or accept Jesus before they are 'saved'. Is **that** not doing something, a work or an action on their part?

The controversy between faith and works is one that Evangelicals have discussed for many years. On one hand, we have *"For by grace are ye saved through faith; and that not of yourselves: it is the gift of God: Not of works, lest any man should boast."* (Ephesians 2:8, 9)

On the other hand *"What doth it profit, my brethren, though a man say he hath faith, and have not works? can faith save him?"* (James 2:14) Let's review the verses that headed this chapter plus . . . add "*. . . (God) who will render to every man according to his deeds . . . Tribulation and anguish, upon every soul of man that doeth evil . . . But glory, honour, and peace, to every man that worketh good . . .*"

(Romans 2:6, 9a & 10a)

Whether we want to admit it or not, faith and works have existed from the Garden of Eden. God gave us FREE WILL, and the MIND with which to use it.

When God made a covenant with a person or His people, it imposed responsibility upon man to behave in certain ways, living according to certain laws or rules of conduct. On the other hand, God's unfailing mercy shined forth despite man's failure. Let us consider these as two threads weaving through the Bible, labeling them —

WORKS / KARMA	FAITH / GRACE
1. Adam and Eve through disobedience to God were banished from the Garden of Eden.	God gives His promise of a way they can return back to Him, a Messianic promise.
2. Man continues to live for himself, not caring and unmindful of God's laws — then the flood.	First covenant established regarding the rainbow after the flood.
3. Man disobeys, goes into slavery.	God, through Moses and Aaron, delivers them from slavery and promises them their own land.
4. God gives the law (10 commandments); they continue to disobey, and wander in the wilderness for 40 years.	Through mercy and forgiveness God protects, guides, feeds, and finally leads them into their own land, 'flowing with milk and honey'. God's enduring love, despite their continued disobedience.
5. Old Testament or Covenant contains all the above.	New Testament or Covenant contains all the above and MORE!
6. Codes, Rules, and regulations provide the blueprint for human behavior.	Law written on the heart prompts obedience and appropriate behavior through love.

Jesus was/**is** the perfect pattern for us to follow ... our way-show-er. He was the 'firstfruits' *"... and that he should be the first that should rise from the dead, and should show light unto the people . . ."* (Acts 26:23) *". . . But now is Christ risen from the dead, and become the firstfruits of them that slept."* (I Corinthians 15:20)

The word 'firstfruits' certainly implies that there will be others, additional 'fruits' ripening and following His example. *"For both he that sanctifieth and they who are sanctified are all one: for which cause he is not ashamed to call them brethren."* (Hebrews 2:11)

Let us consider the verse previous to that listed above *"If in this life only we have hope in Christ, we are of all men most miserable."* (I Corinthians 15:19)

"But now is Christ risen from the dead, and become the firstfruits of them that slept." (I Corinthians 15:20)

11

WHY LEARN OUR LESSON(S) NOW?

". . . behold, NOW is the accepted time; behold, NOW is the day of salvation."

(II Corinthians 6:2b)

One of the great criticisms of the belief in reincarnation is that we can 'eat, drink, and be merry' in this lifetime because we can make up for it the next time around.

Please remember, as a soul matures and postpones needlessly a lesson it needs to learn, the lesson becomes more and more difficult.

If a child does not learn the multiplication tables in one grade of school, the child will find the next grade more difficult when he needs to use that which he should have learned.

God, in His boundless mercy and love, does give us as many lifetimes as necessary to learn our lessons, but each time it is a little more challenge with extra difficulties and handicaps with which to work if we do not learn the necessary lessons.

If you search the deep recesses of your heart, you will realize that there is a part of you that truly wants to **be** the very best, **do** the very best that is possible. That 'conscience' or 'higher self' or Holy Spirit, or whatever you choose to call 'it' is that which is continually prodding you back to your Christ-likeness . . . back to God, your Father, your Source.

Man, in his most depraved self, always yearns and turns to God in times of deep, deep need . . . as did the thief on the cross *"And he said unto Jesus, Lord, remember me when thou comest into thy kingdom."* (Luke 23:42)

You may ask why didn't the other thief (or malefactor as the KJV puts it) turn to Jesus as his way to God? Could it be because he still was trying for the 'easy' way to be removed from his problems or challenges? *"If thou be Christ, save thyself and us."* (Luke 23:39b) He was not ready and willing to return to the Father. Again this is a beautiful example of God's allowing us **FREE WILL**. Truly God is *". . . not willing that any should perish, but that all should come to repentence."* (II Peter 3:9b)

God wants us to have and be ALL that He has promised, but in giving us **FREE WILL**, He wants us to come to Him in LOVE, **not** because that was all we **could** do, but because we **wanted** to do so.

God created man in His image, giving man free will and free choice. God **is** patient and loving. If through **your** choice, you desire to 'stay in the fourth grade' so to speak, many lifetimes . . . then so be it; but I can testify, as can countless others, that if we consider each 'problem' as an 'opportunity' or 'challenge' assisting us in learning our lesson(s), then we are stronger the next time we are presented with a 'problem/challenge' and the joy of victory through Jesus Christ, always gently pulling/guiding us toward God by our becoming more Christ-like is indescribable and satisfying.

How very comforting to know . . .

"There hath no temptation taken you but such as is common to man: but God is faithful, who will not suffer you to be tempted above that ye are able; but will with the temptation also make a way to escape, that ye may be able to bear it."

(I Corinthians 10:13)

"If the Son therefore shall make you free, ye shall be free indeed."

(John 8:36)

"And ye shall know the truth, and THE TRUTH SHALL MAKE YOU FREE."

(John 8:32)

GOD BLESS YOU . . . . .

Our birth is but a sleep and a forgetting
The Soul that rises with us,
Our Life's Star,
Hath had elsewhere its setting,
And cometh from afar;
Not in entire forgetfulness,
And not in utter nakedness,
But trailing clouds of glory do we come
From God, who is our home.

— Wordsworth —

PART II

REINCARNATION
WHO,
WHAT,
WHEN,
WHY,
AND OTHER ANSWERS

Rebirth is no more of a miracle than is birth!

INTRODUCTION — PART II

PART II is not written to convince the skeptics with their lengthy arguments and piles of 'evidence' against reincarnation. There are many, many elaborate volumes and articles written on the subject available for those who wish to seriously investigate the subject.

In PART II, some of the very basic beliefs that more and more Evangelicals are beginning to accept will be set forth. In these few chapters, a presentation of this basic belief is given after my reading and studying many books; having many experiences; through consultations with other questioning Evangelicals; prayer; meditation; and searching the scriptures. Please ask the Holy Spirit *alone* to guide YOU!

Hopefully, this will assist you to an understanding of this awesome, full-of-wonder doctrine, clarifying and explaining disputed points, and summarizing **very briefly** the author's concept of the subject, obtained from many sources.

Perhaps it would be well to issue a word of warning at this point. There are people who become foolish about reincarnation. This is to be expected since every great universal truth or doctrine is sure to be misunderstood or misapplied by those who wish to do so.

Individuals who work with the concept have met **many** who have claimed to be Cleopatra, Joan of Arc, Shakespeare, Napoleon, etc. Just remember, we have **all** had incarnations where we have been ordinary people, living ordinary lives, accomplishing that which we could do best with what we had been given.

We have been (or will be) all colors, creeds, slave or master, rich or poor, famous or infamous. In fact, may I add a word of caution . . . According to my own meditation and study of books, many of which have been authored by advanced souls and authorities on the subject, when you have a particularly strong prejudice against any nationality, or sex . . . beware, your next incarnation may very well be someone in that situation so you will have opportunity to learn the lessons of the 'fruit of the spirit' *". . . love, joy, peace, longsuffering* (patience), *gentleness, goodness* (kindness), *faith, meekness* (humility), *temperance* (self-control). . ." (Galatians 5:22) These are the qualities necessary to bring us back to our Heavenly Father.

Pray about it (prayer is just simply talking to God), ask God to erase that negative feeling from within you, and then do all that you can to assist someone in that category. Really get to know them and find out how they think and feel. If you sincerely pray for forgiveness and desire to eliminate that prejudice, then volunteer to help that person. Perhaps they really didn't want to be what they are in this lifetime, but that was the best way they could learn the lessons with which they needed to be confronted.

Consider also that by learning all you can regarding this seemingly negative situation, your own lesson(s) could be learned or minimized.

If there is a true universal love established or even a great understanding of the situation (aren't most prejudices due to lack of understanding and appreciation of the situation?) then much karma can and will be overcome. One other beautiful truth highly spiritual reincarnationists agree upon is that GRACE ERASES OR MINIMIZES KARMA. Why not try it?

Sometimes we will have 'flashes' or dreams of something, someplace, or someone that seems **very** familiar.

This could be a past life recall, given to assist in times of discouragement, sorrow, etc.

Jesus said "*. . . Thou shalt love the Lord thy God with all thy heart, and with all thy soul, and with all thy mind. This is the first and great commandment. And the second is like unto it,* ***Thou shalt love thy neighbor as thyself.***" (Matthew 22:37-39)

The Evangelicals all agree that this does not mean just your next-door neighbor, but is the kind of universal love that Jesus had. Do you love **all** people as much as you love yourself?

Do you love yourself? . . . Remember, YOU were created in the image and likeness of God, and are the temple of the Holy Spirit.

Please approach PART II with an open mind, asking for the Divine Teacher, the Holy Spirit, to reveal His message to you.

1

WHAT IS REINCARNATION?

Reincarnation is the rebirth of the soul in successive 'human bodies' (See PART I, Chapter 1). A simple doctrine, really, which becomes a natural corollary to that of the immortality of the soul.

Briefly, this doctrine gives the reasons for the method and the proof of the repeated cyclic embodiments on earth in the human form, of the same spiritual being or individual soul.

Therefore, in incarnating, you do not become someone else, but are always the same soul, manifesting in various human bodies, in different circumstances, at different times — just as you dress in different clothes at different seasons of the year.

Reincarnation has as many diverse concepts and shade differences or **great** differences as there are church denominations; differing with the individual's experience, evolutionary progress, open-mindedness, etc. (If the word, evolution bothers you a bit, please see PART III, *SEMANTICS — WHAT DO YOU MEAN BY THAT WORD?)*

I sincerely hope that PART I has whetted your appetite, assisting your own study into the possibility that Reincarnation **could** be a Biblical Doctrine.

I have been contacted by many Evangelicals on all levels in and out of the churches who are interested and desire information on reincarnation that isn't 'far out'. They seek someone who is capable of discussing the subject from their Evangelical background. Someone who can use Bible verses to assist them in their study. In this book, an attempt will be made to use some of my thoughts and understanding of this beautiful doctrine which was presented to them. As we continue to mature and study, we must expect our understanding to grow deeper and become more complex.

For example, consider the Book of Job. Why would God feel it necessary to prove Himself and His power to Satan? Allowing Satan to punish a man so severely, take the lives of his children and servants, and destroy his possessions . . . a man that was, in God's own words from Job 1:1 *". . . perfect and upright, and one that feared (awesome reverence) God and eschewed (to take care to avoid or shun) evil."* A justification for the act of God, in view of His own complementary words of Job, is that Job had to reap what he had sown in a previous lifetime. With this thought, the entire Book of Job takes on the basic theme of reincarnation. The more I studied Job, through the inspiration of the Holy Spirit, the more clearly it explained much about why this very unusual book was included in the Holy Bible.

Doesn't it explain perfectly, *"Whatsoever a man soweth, that shall he also reap"?* (Galatians 6:7b)

It does certainly account for infant or child prodigies, as well as the other end of the spectrum, the infants or children severely handicapped, as will be discussed in greater detail later in this portion of PART II.

It explains the law of justice and that God **does not** create evil nor create souls only to make them suffer: But after we were created in His image, He gave us that wonderful attribute FREE WILL . . . and we have used it!

Many may wonder why the Bible has not clearly taught reincarnation up to this point. Without going into any lengthy discussion of the matter, may it be under consideration that undoubtedly the time was not right. **Now** we should concentrate on the task of achieving our reunion with God instead of postponing this indefinitely as do many Eastern religious people who already DO believe in reincarnation. If not thoroughly understood, this doctrine **may** tend to make people apathetic and fatalistic. The Bible encourages men to seek actively to liberate themselves from all limitations.

NOW is the time. More and more people are beginning

to ask more and more questions. Evangelicals are finding themselves in situations for which their spiritual training cannot and does not provide a satisfactory answer. GOD'S TIME IS **ALWAYS** PERFECT!

As previously mentioned, this is not a new teaching, it has been around for centuries among highly educated and outstanding world leaders, poets, philosophers, etc.

In summation, reincarnation is the rebirth of the soul in successive human bodies. Therefore suggesting a perfect way for the soul to attain all that God has promised and desired for His most unique and remarkable creation.

2

REASONS FOR REINCARNATION

"I have had a hard enough time in this life, I don't want to come back! Is it really necessary?"

Haven't you heard this many times from people when the subject of reincarnation has entered the conversation?

In reply — of course you don't **have** to do anything (remember FREE WILL?), but there is within every soul a desire to return to his Creator, to become again the image of God and after His likeness (Genesis 1:26, 5:1), not desiring to remain in the likeness and image of Adam (Genesis 5:2). This urge may be strong or weak at the present time, but it **is still lurking inside us**, and will surface when man realizes that there MUST be something more, creating a sincere desire to satisfy that longing within.

Our wonderful God is patient and not willing that any should miss out on the opportunity, so He waits . . . and waits . . . . .

It **will** come because:

1. One life is far too short for you to gain the experiences necessary to fulfill the admonition to *"Be ye therefore perfect, even as your Father which is in Heaven is perfect."*

(Matthew 5:48)

2. Each time you come back, you are given the opportunity to learn a major lesson needed to 'round out' your character for the unfolding of your spiritual growth. It may take many lifetimes for one difficult quality/lesson to be presented as will be explained later. Each time you return, you will be confronted with different circumstances, new methods — until the attribute/lesson has been so ingrained or grafted into your soul that you can demonstrate it properly and completely at all times.

3. Then you return to accept the challenge of another attribute or 'fruit of the spirit' (will you please review Galatians 5:22, 23) that you did not learn well or perhaps

have not learned at all. Thereby unfolding the next step in your spiritual maturity to accomplish your great mission of returning to your original created state. Remember, you were given the privilege, opportunity, and responsibility of having dominion over every living thing that is on the Earth (Genesis 1:26-28).

It is your responsibility to train your human self to respond to the guidance of, and express, your spiritual self.

4. You also return to work out the results of past mistakes, reap the rewards of your good deeds, completing the plans unfinished in the past life or lives. As you progress and conquer here and now, you have a lot more control in making yourself whatever you wish to be in your soul's next incarnation.

Could this not be what is meant by the words *"Lay not up for yourselves treasures upon earth, where moth and rust doth corrupt, and where thieves break through and steal: But lay up for yourselves treasures in heaven, where neither moth nor rust doth corrupt, and where thieves do not break through nor steal; For where your treasure is, there will your heart be also."* (Matthew 6:19-21)

Could the 'many mansions' of which Jesus spoke in John 14 be the body you create for yourself to learn the lesson(s) you need to learn in whichever lifetime you will be learning it? Is not a human's body magnificence beyond anyone's comprehension?

5. You return to be with the ones with whom you set up strong ties of love and affection assisting you to neutralize, redeem and secure forgiveness for the enmities, hatreds, and wrongs you had developed with others.

Love and hate are the most binding emotions or forces, therefore, among those 'negative feelings or emotions' it would be wise to *"agree with thine adversary quickly, whilst thou are in the way with him;"* (Matthew 5:25a) in **this** lifetime, or you will be bound to him more closely in another life until you have worked out the disharmony, thereby assisting both of you to progress to the next 'lesson'.

How much different we would look at and treat others if we could and **would** consider this aspect realistically.

6. You return to assist mankind from the curse of impurity and disharmony which their 'sins' have placed upon the lower kingdoms and even upon the atoms of the ground upon which you walk.

As you manifest, embody, and radiate peace, love, joy, harmony, etc., from the Divine Self* within, in **that** proportion, the activity of those spiritual forces purify, uplift, and redeem the atoms of your body and the matter you contact; i.e., you attract to you that which you project, unless, of course, you are given the situation as a challenge for spiritual growth.

*Some Evangelicals will tend to reject my inference that we **all** have the Christ/Divine Self or whatever you wish to call it. Let us reason for a moment. When we recognize a desire so strongly to 'accept' Jesus the Christ and all He stands for, the Holy Spirit comes to stay within us — we are 'born again', have a rebirth, or use the terminology you desire. Yet, Jesus said, "*No man can come to me, except the Father which hath sent me draw him.*" (John 6:44) How can we be drawn by the Father, unless the Holy Spirit is within waiting for the time when we will exercise our FREE WILL to allow ourselves to be drawn.

Please remember, truly our greatest desire is to be like Jesus, the Christ . . . to claim our inheritance of being created in the image and likeness of God, having the dominion we were created to have.

Hopefully that will occur in this lifetime, or has occurred in a previous lifetime. Do we not all know people who just won't accept the concept of Christ, or even God? Yet they are good people. Fear not, dear one, God is patient, and is not willing that any of His most outstanding creation be lost or wasted.

For those who have attained the 'fruit of the spirit' in another lifetime; they have chosen to return to assist others.

I can think of a situation some years ago when five missionaries were killed while trying to help a very primitive tribe of South American Indians. This created quite a stir in Evangelical circles.

One martyred man's wife took her children, against the advice and desire of family and friends and immediately returned to this tribe. Through Divine intervention, this tribe became friendly and receptive to her and other's efforts.

This occurrence inspired many young people to dedicate their lives to this and other primitive tribes, bringing the message of God's love.

Please keep in mind that a radiant spirit, and the manifesting of the 'fruit of the Spirit', as much and as often as you can, uplifts and advances everything with which you come in contact.

Do you not find you tend to become like those with whom you enjoy being associated?

7. You may continue to return until you learn how to utilize all circumstances, emotions, opportunities to complete your mission of building an expression of the spiritual self as perfect as the limitations will permit, subordinating your will to the will of the indwelling Spirit.

8. After you have reached this mastery and no longer need to return to earth for your own advancement *"Him that overcometh will I make a pillar in the temple of my God, and he shall go no more out:"* (Revelation 3:12a), you may voluntarily return out of love and compassion to teach, relieve suffering or otherwise help your fellow men in their progress.

Some examples of famous men of whom this could be said since they served others unselfishly against all odds are Abraham Lincoln, Gandhi, Booker T. Washington, Thomas Edison, Albert Einstein, Dr. George Washington Carver, to name a **very** few. Booker T. Washington and Dr. George Washington Carver, as well as Martin Luther King, assisted their race to strive upward, showing what could be accomplished by the seemingly underprivileged.

Looking on the 'negative' side for a moment, we pass judgment upon ourselves, **and others**, thereby punishing ourselves in countless ways — by overworking, by refusing to care for our magnificent body temple with proper sleep, food, or rest — trying to be a perfectionist (one never is, of course, and there is always someone to remind us that we are not) . . . thereby causing illness. Or by withdrawing from friends and/or family; by doing chores or working at a job we dislike or detest; by letting others impose upon us or accepting all matter of unhappy, unhealthy situations and labeling it 'God's Will'. When III John 2 says *"Beloved, I wish above all things that thou mayest prosper and be in health, even as thy soul prospereth."*

We should not judge ourselves harshly or over-evaluate events in our lives. Realizing that if we came here in this incarnation, for example, to overcome lying and deceit, our lives will be filled with opportunities to lie or not to lie, to deceive or not to deceive, thus assisting us to learn our needed lesson(s) by using our FREE WILL. As James 1:2 states, *"My brethren, count it all joy when you fall into divers* (various) *temptations."*

Just as in any schoolroom, when we need to learn mathematics, for example, we are given all kinds and varieties of problems to assist us to master the subject thoroughly and completely. Therefore, it is logical that our lives will be filled with that which is the most difficult for us to do.

9. Please bear in mind that our lesson(s) can be made easier and our learning swifter by the Grace of God; through Jesus, the Christ, our way-shower; and the teaching and power of the Holy Spirit.

Never underestimate the power of prayer, memorizing the **positive** statements from the Bible, or devising your own positive affirmation. If there is something specific you wish to demonstrate such as: *"I can do all things through Christ which strengtheneth me"* (Phillippians 4:13), and I therefore have the strength to live this day without a cigarette or whatever." For just as light travels 186,000 miles per second; a thought, an intention of a prayer given, is sent even quicker than you can possibly comprehend. God delights in the **prayers of faith** from a much-loved child.

Just as God is more powerful and capable than the adversary, positive thought are MUCH more powerful than negative ones.

3

FREE WILL VERSUS FATE

People often feel that the Doctrine of Reincarnation and karma is fatalistic, thereby destroying the right of the individual to live his own life, overshadowing his daily life and purposes with the building of inevitable circumstances.

Is there such a thing as FREE WILL and what connection does it have with fate? FREE WILL implies that a man can be and do anything he desires. However, man can only do and be that of which he is capable. That which man can conceive, in his heart believe, he can achieve!

The power of choice **is** a tremendous thing, and gives one the privilege of choosing that which appears to be the best from among many possibilities. This power of selectivity is in a sense, **dharma**, or the law of nature; positive thinking, unlimited thinking. The right to interpret and select certain elements from the karma that we have on hand.

For example, it may be karma that you go to live in another state or country; but it is dharma that allows you to choose the means of transportation and to a degree, the place where you will go to live, thus gaining the knowledge and experiences necessary at that point in your life. Having gained the knowledge and experiences from this move, it is your dharma that enables you to use this to advance your own ends. However, it is your inevitable karma to suffer, **if**, in the advancement of your own purposes, you commit any fault against spiritual law.

Please remember that there are always two ways to look at a situation. That which is often construed as 'evil' by one person, may not be 'evil' or 'negative' at all when understood in its proper prospective or in the light of another person's experience. *". . . ye thought evil against me; but God meant it unto good . . ."* (Genesis 50:20) Every person is free to do certain things, but having done them, he must abide by their consequences. THERE CAN BE NO EXCEPTIONS or the whole reasonable universe collapses.

As for fate, it may be fate that we meet certain challenges but it is integrity that we face them well, using them as stepping stones to greater achievement.

Karma brings us into life according to the particular destiny of the entity. Having thus entered this world, we are capable of accomplishing certain actions. We have the FREE WILL to study hard or to be lazy; to be efficient or inefficient; happy or sad; honest or dishonest. As we continue through life we will have the right to react to these karmic conditions as our understanding dictates. Having once started a course of procedure, karma sets in again, and each action begins a new chain of consequences.

No one who is ignorant of any kind of law (God's, state, country, etc.) can possibly be free. True freedom belongs entirely to those who know the laws, obeys them to the best of their ability, thereby emancipating themselves from bondage to retributive karma.

By working out the old and ceasing to create new karma, a person becomes identified with the personality that has achieved perfection.

This results in one who no longer thinks merely with the mind, but rather bears witness to the Father above all else.

Reincarnation is **not** fatalistic. A criminal being caught, does not necessarily associate the punishment for his crime with any system or fatalism, but inwardly yields himself to cause and effect.

Nor does any reckless over-eater consider his dyspepsia as fatalism; he merely recognizes his indiscretion and bemoans the fact that his constitution will not support his appetite.

Remember that fate is merely the final result or consequence, or outcome; and karma is simply the working out of the Biblical teaching *"Be not deceived; God is not mocked: for whatsoever a man soweth, that shall he also reap."* (Galatians 6:7)

4

WHY, WHEREFORE = THEREFORE

Have you ever wondered how a very young boy could compose a symphony at age 7? How an otherwise normal child could sit down at a piano at age 5 and begin playing a simple classic that her tiny fingers could barely master?

Or a boy of extremely poor circumstances would have such devotion to his studies that he reads books by the light of the fireplace in his log cabin home, and even though he never attended law school, nor college, nor was a great orator, became one of the greatest Presidents of all time.

How a very ordinary little black boy was so entranced with the 'lowly' peanut that he became knowledgeable and developed hundreds of uses for the peanut, an inexpensive commodity, that was easily grown and obtained . . . using his knowledge and example to benefit his impoverished people.

Or two children can be born in the same home, of the same parents, having the same love and advantages, yet one becomes an outlaw and the other a respectable citizen?

How a young girl is born, loved so devotedly, lives a pleasant life in lovely surroundings, gets a good education, prepares for a satisfying job and gets one — then after a short time, is found in the woods, raped and murdered, her assailant unknown and not found.

A dear couple, much in love and desiring children, after much praying and expensive doctors' tests, are blessed with the birth of a baby boy ... but soon discover that he is severely retarded.

A lady, who seemingly has everything — a husband who loves and is faithful to her, able to supply the family of children with a lovely home and all they could need or want . . . commits suicide.

A charming, delightful, intelligent young man in college joins the army during wartime to serve his country that he loves; progresses so rapidly and well that he becomes an officer and in his first big battle is killed.

Why would a God of such love and concern for His greatest creation allow wars, famine, torture . . .?

We could go on and on, filling a book with just such questions as the above — but let's see if we can find a possible answer in reincarnation.

Let us consider, for a few moments on a **very basic** level the different bodies we know we have. The **physical** body with which we are well acquainted; the part we see when we look in a mirror — that has pain, suffering, etc. This is also called the conscious body with a conscious mind.

Then there is also the **subconscious** body or the **astral** body. An exact image of the human body, but more subtle, invisible but definitely penetrating every cell of the physical body. For the purpose of this book, let us realize that this astral body never dies, but contains a level of the soul. Could this be the body of Jesus that He made visible appearing to Mary immediately after His resurrection? Remember that He asked Mary that she *". . . Touch me not; for I am not yet ascended to my Father."* (John 20:17a)

We also have a **spiritual** body. It was this body of Jesus that He made visible, although the doors were locked, and said to His disciples *"Peace be unto you."* (John 20:19) He encouraged Thomas (doubting Thomas) to put Thomas' finger in the print of the nails, and thrust his hand into Jesus' side. (John 20:25-31)

Jesus walked on water, and ate fish and bread with some of His disciples after their miraculous catch of fish in John 21:1-14.

The astral and the spiritual body never dies, but lives to reincarnate — as we shall discuss later.

Each soul comes to earth with a purpose and a specific

goal to accomplish, that the soul might be more Christ-like as discussed previously.

To explain more clearly, let us take a family as an example; using the incarnation given through death and thereafter, this gives a broad range of possible events.

By using data from previously published sources, and from individuals whom I have interviewed, whom have had a death, or near-death experience, possible implications are portrayed.

PLEASE UNDERSTAND THIS IS A FICTIONAL COMPOSITE EXAMPLE. WE CAN'T POSSIBLY KNOW WHAT THEIR PREVIOUS LIVES CONTRIBUTED — NOR ALL THE THOUGHTS AND ACTIONS IN THE LIFE PORTRAYED.

The parents will be Archie and Betty and their three children, Harold, Carl, and Sharon.

5

ARCHIE

Archie lived a rather simple, ordinary life. Most of us do live an ordinary, relatively simple life with only the complexities of everyday problems to work with and through.

Archie was a decent man, a fine husband who provided the necessities for his family, and a father who loved his wife and three children, even though he was not very demonstrative.

His family attended church faithfully and gave spasmodically to the church's upkeeping. He really didn't have, expect, or want a personal relationship with God. After all, God had more important things to do than to be particularly interested in Archie and his family.

Yes, Archie believed in Heaven and Hell, but rather thought that he had enough 'points' to make it to Heaven since he did all of the above and tried to live up to the 'Ten Commandments'.

In advancing years, he was not too surprised when he was diagnosed as having a terminal disease, and after a somewhat painful few months, his physical body separated from his astral body (they are held together by a 'silver cord' which is severed at 'death' (Ecclesiastes 12:6), and Archie felt no more pain.

. . . But he was perplexed — he **saw** a body that looked like his body lying on the bed, but looking at himself, he saw what appeared to be the same body some distance away from the bed.

Soon it seemed (time appeared to stand still where Archie felt himself to be), his wife, Betty, entered the bedroom and with dismay, discovered that Archie was lying very still — oh my . . . he is not even breathing . . . and his eyes are open.

She immediately called the doctor and began to cry, for she and Archie had been peacefully contented and she did not want to be left alone.

Archie, still quite confused, but relieved not to have any more suffering, went over to try to comfort her and his other children as they arrived one by one after being contacted.

Much to his amazement, they did not see him, nor hear his words of comfort — in fact, it is as if he was not there. Sharon, his beloved and only daughter, mentions once that she 'feels' Dad's presence. Archie tries to scream to them that he **is** there — feeling great . . . but to no avail.

The doctor came, pronounced him 'dead' and the undertaker took the body. Archie is now aware that his body died — (but he **feels** so very much alive!) and preparations were made for his funeral.

Still very curious, Archie decides to stay around and see who comes and just what goes on. He certainly hopes they sing happy songs at his funeral with an inspirational message because he feels so good and relieved. He remembered the sad songs and the depressing messages usually given at funerals by most ministers.

Archie is still trying to comfort his loved ones, but, except for his daughter, who is more spiritually aware, he is unable to help. Sharon really seems to know he is close by, and her calm, pleasant assurance gives comfort to her mother, brothers, and friends. Oh, how Archie wished he had listened more attentively to the Bible lessons and had really learned how to pray and commune with God.

His physical body is buried and since Archie realizes that he cannot help his loved ones, he decides to just lie down and sleep for awhile in the lovely, lush, and beautiful place in which he found himself. Since he really didn't think much about 'death and dying' previously, he had no particular expectations as to what to do and he felt that he would like to just rest and sleep . . . so he did.

> The time of 'sleep' varies with progression or evolution (See Evolution in PART III, SEMANTICS/GLOSSARY) of the soul and its awareness of what is to occur. It could be years (as we count time) or need not occur at all.

At the appointed time, Archie is 'awakened' and greeted by loved ones who have 'passed over' or 'died' before him. He is delighted to see his precious mother, admired father, eldest brother, aunts and uncles, and friends. (This could have happened immediately at death or even seconds or minutes before — as has been attested by many observers who have been with their dying loved ones.)

After spending a season with them (time is not measured as such in the higher realms, or Heavenlies, but there is no other term we can use in our comprehension), Archie is told that his presence is desired elsewhere. As quickly as he thinks of going there . . . he is!

He finds himself in a mystical room, as if he were in the spirit (Revelation 3:2). Also present are 25 entities (other highly evolved souls with spiritual bodies or elders, as in Revelation 4:2b-4 *". . . and, behold, a throne was set in heaven and one set on the throne. And he that sat was to look upon like jasper and a sardine stone: and there was a rainbow round about the throne, in sight like unto an emerald. And round about the throne were four and twenty seats: and upon the seats I saw four and twenty elders sitting, clothed in white raiment; and they had on their heads crowns of gold."*) that make up what is called the Karmic Board. Their purpose is to assist his soul in its progression or evolution toward becoming the perfect Christ-like being it was intended to be and inwardly desires to be . . . There is such love and peace radiating from their presence.

The spokesman for the group is *"him that sat upon the great white throne"* as recorded in Revelation 20:11; and the 'book of life', assisting in his 'judgment', contains the record of ALL his incarnations.

They are not really judges in the way we usually think of judges. Archie is basically his own judge. They kindly ask him if he has successfully fulfilled the mission he desired to accomplish when he took on his most recent incarnate body.

Archie did remember **then** what he had come to learn in the lifetime just past. Why did he not know during the time he was living that life? The soul (or as we commonly call our conscience) knows and tries to guide you in the way you make your choices — but remember FREE WILL! If you really consciously knew what you should do, it would be like taking an arithmetic test with the answers before you. God does not want robots, but desires that we come back to Him with the yearning and desire to please Him by striving to yield the 'fruit of the Spirit'. (Galatians 5:22, 23).

Archie so wished he had listened to that still small voice, his conscience, which was the guiding of the Holy Spirit.

Yes, **now he remembered** — he had taken on the last physical vehicle to learn to express love, to be more helpful and loving to others. However, he got so caught up in the everyday mundane affairs of daily living, it was just much easier to do that which was expected and no more.

After all, what had they done for him? How much affection had they shown him? He didn't want to 'put anybody out' or to make them feel an obligation to him, nor for him to feel obligated to them, emotionally, financially, or spiritually.

Archie did progress some, because he did what was required without complaining or withdrawing . . . but, oh, the opportunities he missed. He relates all this with just a little prompting from the Karmic Board.

"Could I please have another chance to do better next time? he asked, for he sees the beautiful, glowing countenances of the Karmic Board, and many of his loved ones, as well as others in passing who have attained more Christ-like qualities — even having seen Jesus, Himself.

The Karmic Board smiles and reminds him that, of course, that is God's desire — that he be like Him. But perhaps, if he would like, he may go to a special teacher, or school of learning in the Heavenlies, where he would be taught more about how to express love, the all encompassing emotion that is the basis of that which IS Christ. Archie wholeheartedly agrees, (FREE WILL, remember?) and he is assigned one that is believed best for him.

As 'time' passes (again this could be what might be termed several years to hundreds of years as more and more a realization of how much that training was really needed), Archie feels he is now ready to try again; to take up a body and return to Earth (the schoolroom of our particular galaxy for testing and trying the lessons we are learning and/or need to learn).

He decides that besides learning to express love and serving God, he would also like to learn patience and tolerance, so he chooses to come back to earth (possibly) as a retarded child.

Have you ever noticed how much love is exuded from most retarded children and/or adults? They also have to be patient because they are handicapped and cannot do that which others easily can; some tolerance is needed because many times they are put into groups where there are others of different races, creeds, degrees of handicap, etc.

Archie learns that he needs to return to parents that require the lessons of patience, love and tolerance also; thus, this will be a special learning experience for all of you. THERE ARE NO ACCIDENTS.

You, and your parents, may learn your lessons early in life, or in your adult life — so you are healed. (Consider John 9.) Jesus told His disciples that *"neither hath this man sinned, nor his parents"* (verse 3) . . . could Jesus have meant 'in this lifetime'? It seems difficult to explain his being blind from birth, since he nor his parents had sinned UNLESS it was pertaining to past lives. Remember, *"whatsoever a man soweth,* ***that*** *shall he also reap."* (Galatians 6:7b)

This, of course, is a **very** narrow example since previous incarnations determine how strongly the man previously referred to as Archie and/or his parents needed the lessons of love, patience, tolerance, etc.

One wonderful (full of wonder) realization is that we are all distinct individuals. We each have our own set of challenges for those certain qualities we have conquered in full or in part.

Let's take another example, Archie's wife, Betty.

6

BETTY

Betty was a vivacious, charming, church-going young girl when she met her 'knight in shining armor' at the age of 19.

She had received excellent training at home, and was anxious to become a loving wife and mother, so she and Archie became engaged and married in due time.

The happy couple were delighted when they realized they were to become parents, and very pleased with their first son whom they named Harold. Within a reasonable time, another son, Carl, arrived . . . then a much desired, eagerly awaited girl, Sharon.

Betty was a devoted mother and faithful wife. Attending a good Bible believing, Bible teaching church, she tried to live her life according to Proverbs 31:10-31 regarding a 'virtuous woman'.

Most certainly she did not want to go to 'Hell' and according to the very strict teaching in her church, that's the way THEY interpreted the Bible. Of course, they did not condone any line of thought that was not according to every 'jot and title' of the Bible (King James Version, naturally). After all, the minister and those who came for special meetings had gone to the very best colleges and seminaries . . . their entire lives were spent studying and teaching what they were taught in those outstanding schools which were created for that very purpose.

Certainly Betty knew nothing about the original languages of the Bible, nor did she even contemplate the many elements involved in the translations, versions, or the councils that met to make certain corrections, additions, or subtractions to the Bible that were more in line with the teaching of the church. In fact, her church rather leaned to the belief that those who talked so much and sang songs about the Holy Spirit were a bit radical.

She was not encouraged to do much reading of the Bible and studying on her own. Weren't the ministers and special speakers supposed to interpret correctly all that was written in the Holy Bible. It was deemed too difficult for the average person to comprehend. That was why the ministers and evangelists went to their Bible schools and seminaries to learn the 'correct' interpretation of the scriptures.

Yes, she did sometimes wonder why there were so many different denominations and beliefs that supposedly came from the same Bible.

Besides, she didn't have time, with her household duties, shopping, three delightful children to care for, sewing, working in and for her church, etc. . . .

She thought much about death after Archie died and began to realize that it could come to her at any time. Her physical body was getting 'old' everyone kept reminding her, and certain organs did not seem to be performing as well as she wished they would; but what could she expect, she had enjoyed her marriage, her children and grandchildren, and she **was** 'old' in age.

Her eldest son, Harold, had grown into a fine young man with a lovely wife and several children. In fact, Harold lived next door and farmed the land since Archie died. Her precious daughter, Sharon, married the Youth Pastor of their church and also had a couple of adorable children. Yes, Betty had a good life.

Her only regret was her second son, Carl. Poor, dear Carl . . . he was so difficult to handle; belligerent, resenting any form of reprimand. He never wanted to go to church, always seemed to be angry about something — **anything**. Betty wondered where she had gone wrong in rearing that intelligent, precious (in a mother's eyes ALL her children are precious) boy.

When she received the news that Carl had been killed in action while serving his country in the army, she really hoped he had accepted Christ before that happened. If he hadn't, according to the teaching of her church, . . . and the minister had stated outright that he was afraid that Carl had gone to Hell.

As she thought more and more on these things, it seemed almost to break her heart — she had nothing to live for anyway. She was so tired and old! It might be better to die and be able to rest her tired body. Her pastor told her many times that she would go to Heaven. Her dear Archie had looked so peaceful in the casket.

One day as she was sitting in her rocker, contemplating her life, and especially regarding Carl, she felt a deep pain . . . she had a heart attack. Immediately she felt such peace and contentment — no pain. She seemed to be looking down on her tired, slumped-over body. Harold came in to check on her as he often did during his work day . . . but he seemed so disturbed because she couldn't seem to be able to answer him when he called or even shook her — her body just wouldn't respond AT ALL . . . she seemed to be separated from it.

Harold immediately called Emergency, but she was declared dead on arrival at the hospital. She didn't feel dead, she felt great! There seemed no way for her to get that across to those precious loved ones, relatives and neighbors who were mourning.

PLEASE DON'T MOURN! She tried to tell them she felt better and younger than she had felt for many years, but they seemed to be totally unaware of HER. They seemed to be around a body that looked like hers — why, she supposed she was dead, at least her body was . . . but she was not!

The instant this realization came to her, she felt herself seeming to float down a long tunnel. It was not an unpleasant experience because there was such beautiful music — as if angels were welcoming her to Heaven. At the end of the tunnel (or some people experience a lovely hallway) she saw a brilliant light, and all around were loved ones whom she recognized had preceeded her in death — but they all looked so very much alive, happy, joyful and loving as she felt. Why, . . . there was her dear Archie.

After she was lovingly greeted, the others slowly left her with Archie and she questioned him about what happened next. Archie asked her what was her heart's desire. She replied a little home for her and Archie with a small flower garden with all colors and varieties of flowers. No sooner had she uttered those words than they appeared just as she had pictured them in her mind.

She also wanted to see her beloved Jesus, and lo . . . He appeared before her just as she had seen Him in pictures on earth. Overwhelmed, she began to kneel before Him, but He reminded her that only God, Himself, was worthy of such worship and adoration. He blessed her and vanished. Beautiful singing and praises were still being heard in the background . . . angels? . . . others who proceeded her? It was so beautiful.

They (Archie and Betty) went into 'her' house, and she asked Archie, "What do we do now?" Archie smiled and replied that he was waiting for her to ask, and that now she no longer needed him, he would leave and someone else would come with a sweet, gentle presence to take her to where she should go.

Immediately it was so — and she found herself standing before 25 of the most loving and wise-looking men. (Revelation 4:2-4)

7

CARL

Carl being the second son, and the middle child, really felt he was dealt a raw deal. Of course, his parents doted on his taller, more attractive, charming and more studious elder brother, while Carl was just an ordinary, plain boy that was born two years after his elder brother.

Then Carl just managed to get himself 'settled in' when three years later, his mother brought home a cute, cuddly, loving and lovable baby **girl**.

He had an ordinary childhood, with all those things against him, constantly following in his brother's footsteps, being compared to his brother and his 'adorable' sister. So when the opportunity came along just before he graduated from high school (in the lower half of his class), he joined the army. Since the country was at war, Carl became an overnight hero. Strong, healthy, and in uniform, for the first time in his rather belligerent life, he felt he was important. The small community in which he lived gave a going-away party for the boys that were leaving — the girls really **noticed him** . . . and WOW, LIFE **could** be great!

His mother and dad, brother and sister (who really did love him) even cried when the time came for him to leave, and some of the girls gave him passionate kisses and told him they were sorry he was going, but "be sure and call when he came home on leave". Carl was glad his elder brother, Harold, could not serve his country in this way because their father was already showing signs of weakness, and someone was needed to tend to the large farm that provided the good living for the family and whose crops would be so needed during this critical time.

Basic camp was certainly not the most pleasant place to be, but as time went on, he responded so well to the army that in due time, he became a Sargent . . . and what a pleasure he got out of telling those new guys what to do and how to do it! He never liked to take orders and now he had an opportunity to **give** some — as well as punishment if things didn't proceed as he wanted.

He particularly hated black men who were so easygoing (Carl said they didn't have the 'guts' to stand up for themselves). **He** made them 'toe the line' and would certainly try to get some 'guts' into them . . . and those black girls were so sensuous; he delighted in sexually mistreating and humiliating them.

To war (overseas) they went, his entire company, and he even enjoyed the combat. This was the exciting life, kill them before they killed you . . . and Carl relished every hard, seemingly endless day of it. Until . . . one day he stepped on a land mine, and after hours and hours of agony and screaming, along with some of his other buddies, he felt no pain — in fact, he felt so light and pleasant it was unbelievable.

He looked around and saw many of his buddies in the same situation. One body appeared to be lying on the battlefield, bloody, battered, and screaming in pain, yet, in the next instant, there seemed to be another body seemingly transparent, standing where he (Carl) was, just as confused and yet quite relieved.

Soon Carl was greeted and hugged by his Grandfather, whom he loved dearly, and was the only one that seemed to understand him as a child — but Carl knew his Grandfather had 'died' a few years before. Then he noticed that his other buddies were also being greeted by loved ones that looked so happy and peaceful.

What a joyous reunion!

Then they all started to walk toward a beautiful, iridescent, shimmering light. Carl's Grandfather started to accompany him, and they walked for a distance, then Carl said, "NO, I want to go back!" Grandfather tried to explain that Carl's time was up for that period on Earth, and this was as it was supposed to happen.

Carl, by this time, was feeling again the hatred for those whom he fought, and those black men especially that he could rule over. **He wanted to go back!**

He met his loving Grandmother, and other loved ones, but his only thought was hate and of the power over those whom he could control. No pleasant sleep for him. Yes, this was a beautiful place, and all the people seemed to look so happy and peaceful, but that only infuriated him more. Why should they be so happy, when he had been so miserable on Earth. He'd show them!

Finally, in love and concern, his Grandfather told him that he must appear before the Karmic Board.

"Well, where is it, let's get it over with." And there he was!

The 25 loving, patient, kind entities tried to talk to him, to request that he go to a place where he could learn to love, not hate, or perhaps a special teacher to assist him in his progress.

But Carl demanded that he be allowed to go back to Earth IMMEDIATELY — okay, if he must be born again, then so be it, but he would sure get at those 'blacks'. Since he had to go back as a baby, he wanted to be the firstborn to parents that loved him most!

The Karmic Board consulted, and since he had FREE WILL, they told him he could have the first available body to be born in the circumstances he requested.

Carl turned on his heel and left . . . and found himself screaming and crying, being placed on his new mother's breast. Her firstborn, so desired by his parents who already loved him devotedly. Yes, this precious baby would have things a bit difficult as a black baby . . . and, oh yes, they would name her Carlynn.

8

SHARON

Sharon had a grand, loving childhood. There was no doubt that it was special having two big, handsome elder brothers. She really loved them both in very different ways. Harold, the eldest, was always so brilliant and kind to her — and she even loved Carl, who continually teased and tormented her. While Harold was so funny and laughed often, Carl rarely seemed to appreciate jokes, and felt they were all against him, and even Sharon couldn't cheer him up . . . and she really tried.

Her mother and father, while loving them all, of course, seemed to delight in their little girl. Her Dad, who wasn't very affectionate, would sometimes take her on his lap and tell her stories, giving her a hug when no one was watching.

When her family would be angry and raise their voices, Sharon would feel sad and tried to be the peacemaker.

Even as a very little girl, she felt God had a special job for her to do. She loved to go to church, even to the church of her friends. Usually, her parents would let her go with her friends to their church, after all, what difference did it make, they all used the same Bible.

Sharon tried to tell her family that there really was a difference. Some of the churches talked much more about God's love, and Jesus, the Christ, who gave the great commandment *". . . Thou shalt love the Lord thy God with all thy heart, and with all thy soul, and with all thy mind . . . and thy neighbor as thyself."* (Matthew 26:37, 39b)

Also, *"A new commandment I give unto you, That ye love one another; as I have loved you, that ye also love one another."* (John 13:34) Love was SO important!

Her family just smiled and thought about the sweet, loving child she was and how proud they were of her. She especially tried to tell Carl about God's love, but he would just retort, "look who's talking, everybody loves you, nobody loves me." Sharon always replied that she loved him as did his entire family, but Carl rejected this.

Sharon continued to read the Bible and go to the special classes where she learned more about her loving, kind, patient, and JUST God . . . not the God of anger that so many people feared.

Then her precious dad became ill with a painful terminal disease. Oh, how she tried to tell him what she had learned but his reply was, in essence, "Why would a loving God do this to me, when I have tried to live right?"

Then his body died.

When Sharon heard about his death, she immediately went to her mother, and as a young teenager, tried to comfort her and her brothers. In fact, she really felt at times that she could smell Dad's pipe, and when she would close her eyes, she could almost hear him saying, "I'm here, Sharon, I'm here!"; but when she opened her eyes — she would just see her mother, brothers, other relatives, and friends.

At the funeral, she felt her Dad's presence very strongly; alive, vibrant, almost youthful, but she knew by now that it would be useless to say anything to the others.

She did remember all she had been taught, all that had been recorded in her heart, and realized that there is no death . . . and she had peace.

In fact, others could hardly understand why this loving sensitive girl was not mourning as loudly and deeply as her mother and brothers. She felt like standing up in that mournful service and shouting, "But he's not dead, just that painful, tired body is dead . . . Dad lives on."

Sharon was soon teaching a Sunday school class, no, not in the same church her parents had attended, but one that taught the LOVE message of Jesus, the Christ. She sang in the choir and did everything to serve her Lord.

She married a loving husband, in fact, he was the Youth Pastor of the church. They had normal, active children, and all became more and more involved in teaching and practicing the love of God as so beautifully exemplified in Jesus Christ.

Time passed, and after many years of serving the Lord, nothing extremely special or outstanding happened; she just provided dedicated, prayful, loving service to her family, her church, her community, and all with whom she came in contact . . . Sharon had a heart attack one night and just slept away.

As she looked down and saw her body lying on the bed, she immediately heard a sweet, small voice saying "That's alright, Sharon, it is time." She saw a beautiful, shimmering white light before her — it seemed to be the presence of Christ — oh, how she wanted to see Him. He appears as she had pictured Him in her heart.

Immediately she felt — no, she actually saw her beloved Dad, her precious Mother, and . . . other loved ones coming toward her. She was surrounded with such love; indescribably beautiful music, and brilliant colors.

What a joy to be back. Yes, back, for she recognized that she had been there many times before . . .

Soon (?) she appeared before the Karmic Board. As they lovingly asked, "Sharon, did you accomplish what you wanted to do in that lifetime?" she saw her life flash before her and realized that yes, she had wanted to go back and help teach and live the love of God.

Perhaps she had not been as tolerant as she might have been with those who did not desire or even try to love and please God. She had been quite angry at the people who had started the war in which her dear brother, Carl, had been killed, for she truly did love him. She had lived such a protected life, and found it difficult to accept and love those people.

"Please may I learn how to love more universally and be more tolerant as Jesus Christ was?" she asked.

The Karmic Board smiled and recommended a place for additional learning and training with special teachers where she would be assisted to exemplify the Christ love.

Sharon had already learned much in her other lifetimes, and was getting closer to being one with Jesus, her Elder Brother, as she became one with the Father. *"That they all may be one; as thou, Father, art in me, and I in thee, that they also may be one in us."* (John 17:21)

9

SUMMARY

As with most laws of nature, the law of reincarnation is simple in outline but extremely complicated in detail.

You, the real YOU, your soul, is very complicated.

Child prodigies are always souls who have acquired their proficiency or skills in a previous lifetime . . . and notice that they are usually born into an environment or with a family that is favorable or at least sympathetic to them and/or their particular skills or talents.

How much more tolerable we would be with others if we realized that their circumstances were for a purpose — as is ours.

At one time or another I'm sure you have met a person that you instantly disliked and yet do not know any reason for that reaction. Could it be that this person is or reminds you of someone with whom you have a lesson to learn. OR, an individual or group you come in contact with, and instantly a beautiful, satisfying and loving relationship is formed. Perhaps this was a special person or group sent your way to assist you with their love and understanding in your particular challenge at this time . . . and have been connections from another lifetime.

A husband/wife relationship is the closest one that possibly exists, and the spouses are souls that have had many incarnations together in many types of relationships. This extremely close relationship affords us a marvelous opportunity to work out much karma.

Have you ever noticed that it is rare for a husband and wife to be extremely similar in their habits and tastes, desire, etc. If the husband is a 'day' person, his wife is a 'night' person; if he likes sports, she prefers cultural things. If he is extremely methodical and neat, she is more casual. Of course, these are extremes and may vary to degrees, but rarely are they totally and completely in one accord. Opposites **do** attract!

What an opportunity for spiritual growth, to really learn the 'fruit of the spirit'. (Galatians 5:22, 23)

There are occasions where a marriage should never have taken place at all (remember FREE WILL), but since it **did** occur, attempt to do your part to learn all you and your partner can in that outstanding relationship before you consider dissolving it, and your reactions may help you more than you realize as you progress or evolve.

Have you also noticed how many times a person will divorce a spouse for a particular reason, then soon he/she has married another person with almost the identical traits? The lesson has not been learned!

Most reincarnationists believe that the soul experiences life as a male and a female, because the lessons and challenges of both sexes must be learned to truly be understanding, patient, and tolerant. It is much easier to gain the knowledge needed compatible with the male characteristics when a male, and vice versa. The same is true with all races, colors, circumstances, etc.

On this point, as with some other differentiations, I am willing to rest in the knowledge that God, in His omniscience (all-knowledge) and omnipotence (all-power) will perform that good work in me that He began.

"Being confident of this very thing, that he which hath begun a good work in you will perform it until the day of Jesus Christ." (Phillipians 1:6)

"That they all may be one; as thou, Father, are in me, and I in thee, that they also may be one in us: that the world may believe that thou has sent me."

"And the glory which thou gavest me I have given them; that they may be one, even as we are one:"

"I in them, and thou in me, that they may be made perfect in one; and that the world may know that thou hast sent me, and hast loved them, as thou hast loved

me." (John 17:21-23)

EVERYTHING is in DIVINE ORDER for the child of God who sincerely and earnestly desires to be like Christ . . . PERFECT!

I sincerely trust and pray that PART II has opened your mind even slightly . . . or has assisted in answering some questions you may have asked. God is MUCH GREATER and more MAGNIFICENT than most Evangelicals believe Him to be!

Jesus Christ, in every way our perfect 'way-show-er' *". . .I am the way, the truth, and the life: no man cometh unto the Father, but by me."* (John 14:6) . . . HE IS THE CHRIST! *"Thou art the Christ, Son of the living God. And Jesus answered and said unto him, Blessed art thou, Simon Bar-jona; for flesh and blood hath not revealed it unto thee, but my Father which is in Heaven."* (Matthew 16:16b, 17)

The Holy Spirit, our precious companion, comforter, and teacher expand to unlimited dimension as we realize all that He (the Holy Spirit) is. Please remember the Holy Spirit is one member of the Triune God. *"That they all may be one; as thou, Father, art in me, and I in thee, that they also may be one in us: that the world may believe that thou has sent me."* (John 17:21) Please review Jesus' beautiful prayer in John 17.

May you continue to study under the guidance and teaching of the Holy Spirit ONLY!

REINCARNATION — A BIBLICAL DOCTRINE?

PART III

SEMANTICS / GLOSSARY

Do **you** mean what **I** mean when a word is used?

The question is not only what does the word mean, but what does the person using and the person hearing or reading it perceive the word to mean.

God doesn't have to put His name at the end of a rainbow, because nobody else makes rainbows.

—unknown

INTRODUCTION TO PART III

Normally, a glossary is not meant to be read in a prose fashion. This glossary is different. It is suggested that it be read as it contains additional information and scriptural references to bridge the divergence of thinking between reincarnation and traditional teachings.

Some of the words have been used in the previous two parts, others have not been utilized but were included to add a further dimension to these wonderful truths.

When I first began my quest for answers to the many Bible questions that kept coming to my mind — and in reading books toward which I was led by the Holy Spirit — or attending conferences and seminars where my mind was challenged to be more open; I found a different vocabulary. Perhaps they said the same word with which I was familiar, but they seemed to have a slightly different shade of meaning to it.

I also noticed that some teachers/books shied away from using words with which I was accustomed. Seemingly the word had lost its true meaning in overuse, or the emphasis seemed a bit misplaced. A good example is the phrase 'born-again Christian'. Any Biblical student knows that if a person is born-again, they are a Christian, but due to much adverse publicity in the past few years, the term has been one of ridicule instead of joy.

There is an old and true ancient saying: *"When the pupil is ready, the teacher is there."* And as you might expect, God, in His infinite wisdom, led me to teachers and books whose authors had much the same type of Biblical background as mine.

Yet I didn't really understand their language. How I longed for a book or a portion of a book which I could use to learn what THEY meant. I KNEW the Evangelical definition of the words, but they had a slightly different 'shade' to the meaning of the words, or the words were entirely foreign to me.

I hesitated to interrupt the class or seminar to ask any questions, or even approach the teacher later.

Through much study, as well as my own meditation and asking the Holy Spirit to teach me, the following words and meanings have been gleaned.

Many of these words have not been used in this book, but probably will be encountered as you read other material, so they are included to assist you in your own study as directed by the Holy Spirit.

Since there are entire books written about some of these subjects or words, this 'glossary' will only attempt to give a brief summary to acquaint you with the word or phrase. Scripture references are given when possible to aid you in connecting the word with your present understanding.

Dictionary definitions used in this portion are taken from *WEBSTER'S NEW WORLD DICTIONARY* of the American Language Concise Edition, published by The World Publishing Company, Cleveland and New York, unless otherwise noted with an asterick (*).

GLOSSARY

ADEPT (a-dept') — one highly skilled; proficient, i.e., "he is adept in Bible knowledge . . . an advanced thinker or one who sees beyond the readily apparent higher Truth."

AKASHA (a-kash'-a) — known in Evangelical circles as the "Book of Life" is referred to in Revelation 20:12, in which every thought, word, and action in the material world is recorded. However, the Akasha includes information regarding ALL lives lived on Earth. A complete history of the soul.

ALTAR (all'-tar) — a stabilized place of worship. The place in consciousness where we meet the Lord and are willing to give up our lower nature and personal desires for the highest which is the 'fruit of the spirit'. *"But the fruit of the Spirit is love, joy, peace, longsuffering, gentleness, goodness, faith, Meekness, temperance: against such there is no law."* (Galatians 5:22, 23)

The true altar symbolizes the consciousness of full consecration that takes place first in the temple of worship within: *"I beseech you therefore, brethren, by the mercies of God, that ye present your bodies a living sacrifice, holy, acceptable unto God, which is your reasonable service."* (Romans 12:1)

ANGEL — one of an order of spiritual beings endowed with immortality, attendant upon God. A heavenly guardian, ministering spirit, or messenger.

APOCALYPSE (a-poc'-a-lypse) — disclosure of revelation. A name frequently given to the last book of the Bible, **REVELATION**.

AQUARIAN AGE (a-qwar'-e-an) — the age in which we are now living. This age will be one of increasing understanding of spiritual Truths. Prejudices will fall away as we realize that *"And God said, Let us make man in our image, after our likeness: and let them have do-*

minion over the fish of the sea, and over the fowl of the air, and over the cattle, and over all the earth, and over every creeping thing that creepeth upon the earth. So God created man in his own image, in the image of God created he him; male and female created he them." (Genesis 1:26, 27) When we truly realize that ALL men are created equal without thought of color or creed. . .then the true teachings of Jesus' will be clearly revealed on many levels according to capability of comprehension.

ARCHANGEL (ark'-an-gel) — an angel of the highest rank (there are known to be only seven Archangels).

ARMAGEDDON (Ar-ma-ged'-don) — a prophetic battlefield where the kings of the world will supposedly gather together unto the war of the great day of God. (Revelation 16:16)

ASCENDED MASTERS — highly evolved souls, who desire to incarnate to assist in an outstanding way the evolution of a country, a race, or a group of people, thus assisting the entire world.

For example; Gandhi, so loved by his people that he brought peace to a very warlike area in a very warlike time — just by fasting and praying; Abraham Lincoln, George Washington Carver, and others.

ASTRAL BODY (as'-tral) — a replica, though invisible, of the visible human body. It is very subtle, never needing sleep or rest; in fact, it is most active when the physical body rests, sleeps, or is otherwise incapacitated (through illness, etc.). For the purpose of this book, the astral body is the recepticle of the soul. The astral body can also be two-fold. The lower astral, the psychic, which is not necessarily spiritual; while the 'higher astral' is already on a spiritual path, regardless of how much a beginner they are or their level of awareness. (See **HIGHER SELF.**)

The sincere, spiritual Evangelical is already on a spiritual path, as they open their mind and heart to deeper teachings, they are just 'shifting into a higher gear' so to speak.

The astral body sometimes travels during sleep; i.e., when you have experienced the delight of 'seeing' a loved one of whom you have recently thought, or for whom you have prayed; or you have visited or helped needy people in what seemed to be a 'dream'. The astral body is connected to the physical body by a **SILVER CORD**. (Ecclesiastes 12:6)

AURA (aur'a) — an electromagnetic force field of energy that surrounds any living thing. Thoughts, feelings, and health are registered in this force field, which is seen as colors by someone very sensitive to the true spiritual aspect of this force field. Very often seen by children who, of course, believe that everyone can see auras — until, as they grow older, they lose this ability; unless they allow themselves to maintain this ability or become sensitive again.

Also, an aura can be very often felt, as when you are in the presence of a person and you 'feel' a sadness, a happiness, or a health situation without knowing what it is that is making you feel that way.

Actually, since all 'solid' objects are not really solid at all, but have millions of atoms in constant motion being held together by an invisible force, even inanimate objects have an aura of their own, seen as blue-white.

Prayer liberates the energies pent up in the mind and body. Moses, after praying on Mount Sinai *"And when Aaron and all the children of Israel saw Moses, behold, the skin of his face shone; . . . And till Moses had done speaking with them, he put a vail on his face."* (Exodus 34: 30, 33)

Luke testifies that when Jesus was praying *"his countenance was altered, and his raiment was white and glistering."* (Luke 9:29)

In many of the older pictures of Jesus and His Mother, Mary, the artist has used a halo of light around their heads, usually white, sometimes gold, sometimes both. This was the way the artist had of expressing the aura, which during meditation on the painting and what he wanted to express, perhaps was actually seen in his mind's eye; for a highly sensitive artist sees things that the average individual is not trained to observe.

AWARENESS i.e., **SPIRITUAL AWAKENING** — becoming conscious of your spiritual need of God . . . that there must be more! . . . the need of being 'born-again'.

BORN-AGAIN — THE AWARENESS OF ALL THAT GOD IS AND ALL THAT MAN IS NOT! Therefore, the desire to attain the standards that God has set for us, through the example of Jesus Christ. Man becomes lifted above the thoughts of the world and into a heavenly realm. He is truly a new creature desiring to radiate the 'fruit of the Spirit'. (Galatians 5:22, 23)

The realization of a soul to a consciousness of his unity with the one God. It comes here and now. Jesus made no mention of resurrection after death as having part in the new birth. In fact, He said *"Except a man be born again, he cannot see the kingdom of God."* (John 3:3b) (Also, see **CONVERSION** and **NEW BIRTH**.)

CHAKRA (shaw'kra) — Sanskrit for wheel. There are seven (7) major chakras, or centers of light, governing the flow of energy to the physical and astral bodies. Each is known to have a different vibratory rate with a corresponding sound and color . . . and a function in the development of the Higher Self.

CHANNEL — a person who allows himself to serve as a link between the human level and a higher evolved and/or Divine Source. Every true spiritual teacher realizes that when they teach (or preach) they feel a greater power than their own speaking through them. Many times they find themselves adding Biblical quotations, examples, or quotations from books written by great teachers, that they had not previously planned — adding much to that which they had intended.

Or they (the spiritual teacher or preacher) may feel 'led' as they face their audience to change their subject matter altogether and the words just flow from their lips. The Evangelicals recognize this as the power of the Holy Spirit. The teacher is merely a Channel . . . or a Medium, or a go-between. This can be done through clairaudience, clairsentience, clairvoyance or a combination of them. (See **MEDIUM**.)

CHELA (che'(as in cheek)-la) — a pupil, a disciple brought up in the house or school of spiritual instruction, taught by a special spiritual teacher. Also spelled cheela.

CHERUBIM — one of an order of angelic being in the celestial hierarchy whose particular purpose is to protect. For example, the cherubim were placed at the east of the garden of Eden, to keep the way of the tree of life (See Genesis 3:24). Regarding the sacred Ark of the Covenant *". . . thou shalt make a mercy seat of pure gold . . . and thou shalt make two cherubims of gold . . . one cherub on one end, and the other cherub on the other end . . .and the cherubims shall stretch forth their wings on high, covering the mercy seat with their wings, and their faces shall look one to another . . . and there I (God) will meet with thee, and I will commune with thee from above the mercy seat, from between the two cherubims which are upon the ark . . ."* (See portions of Exodus 25:17-22)

CHRIST — the incarnating principle of the God-man; the Perfect Word. *"In the beginning was the Word, and the Word was with God, and the Word was God. The same was in the beginning with God . . . And the Word was made flesh, and dwelt among us, (and we beheld his glory, the glory as of the only begotten of the Father,) full of grace and truth."* (John 1:1-2, 14)

Jesus is the name representing an individual expression of the Christ idea. Christ, the God-like, Divine being, existed long before Jesus, the man. It was the Christ Mind in Jesus that exclaimed *"And now, O Father, glorify thou me with thine own self with the glory which I had with thee before the world was."* (John 17:5)

Christ abides in each person as his potential perfection. Jesus Christ, the embodiment of all Divine ideas, exists eternally as the only begotten Son of God, the 'Messiah' or 'Anointed One', and is the living Principle working in men.

Christ is the visible manifestation of the Messiah.

CHRISTIAN — one who lives and teaches the principles and teachings of Jesus, the Christ; especially as taught directly through Jesus, i.e., The Sermon on the Mount (Matthew 5:7), the greatest commandments (Matthew 22:36-40), as well as His other teachings. *". . . And the disciples were called Christians first in Antioch."* (Acts 11:26b)

CLAIRAUDIENCE (clair-aud'-e-nce) — (Fr. clair = clear), audience — the act or the power of hearing something not present to the ear but regarded as having objective reality.* Most have experienced this at some time or other when they have actually heard a voice speaking to them, and in looking around could see no one. Many times this is a warning of extreme danger, or when needing special comfort or guidance. Some Biblical examples of clair-audience are (1) when Philip was told by an angel of God (visible or invisible?) to go toward the south . . . into Gaza . . . then join himself to the chariot of the Ethopian eunuch (See Acts 8:26-31); and (2) Saul's experience as he journeyed to Damascus. (See Acts 9:4-8). Even the men with Saul *"stood speechless, hearing a voice, but seeing no man."* (verse 7)

CLAIRSENTIENCE (clair-sen'-te-nce) — perception of what is not normally perceptible* being sensitive to intuitive guidance or just intuitively knowing what to do. Example: *"He (Jesus) left Judea, departed again unto Galilee. And he must needs go through Samaria."* (John 4:3, 4)

Also, the story of Ananias and Sapphira as recorded in Acts 5:3. Peter knew they were lying — not only to him, but to God through the Holy Spirit.

When Paul was preaching and Eutychus slept, fell out the window *". . . and was taken up dead. And Paul went down, and fell on him, and embracing him said, Trouble not yourselves; for his life is in him . . . And they brought the young man alive, and were not a little comforted."* (See Acts 20:9b-12.)

CLAIRVOYANCE (clair-voy'-nce) — ability to perceive matters beyond the range of ordinary perception*. The gift of being able to see that which is not visible to the ordinary human eye. Seeing the aura is a form of clairvoyance. Example: Saul's experience when *"suddenly there shined round about him a light from heaven."* (Acts 9:3b) The Bible does state that men which journeyed with him heard a voice, but does not state that they saw anything. (See Acts 9:7.)

There are many examples of people in the Bible seeing visions that prophesied and acted upon their visions and God's will was accomplished.

CONSCIENCE — a knowledge or feeling of right or wrong, with a compulsion to do right; moral judgment that opposes the violation of a previously recognized ethical principle.

CONSCIOUSNESS — the state of being aware, especially of what is happening around one in the physical plane . . . the totality of one's thoughts, feelings, and impressions: mind.

EXPANDED CONSCIOUSNESS — enlarging the conscious mind through learning, especially (for the purpose of this book) in a spiritual sense.

This awareness, or knowing, is very important to spiritual growth. Divine ideas must be incorporated into our consciousness before they can mean anything to us; intellectual concepts do not suffice.

CONVERSION — to change; transform, turn around. When one is 'converted' one merely decides to change from being (for example) a very negative person to becoming a positive person; to see the good in people and circumstances instead of looking for the 'bad' in the situation . . . or to turn from the 'evil or destructive' thoughts and acts to seeking the path of righteousness and/or practicing the teachings of the Christ/Messiah.

A real experience of determining your desire to have a new life in Christ-consciousness; beginning, through the exercise of your mind in thinking about God and His law of love, to travel the path by becoming a new creature in Christ Jesus. (See **BORN AGAIN** and **NEW BIRTH**.)

COSMIC (kos'-mic) — the universe at large as a harmonious system, perfect in order and arrangement. Cosmic is the adjective, COSMOS is the noun.

CROSS — the greatest and most powerful of all symbols; in essence, (spiritually, of course) the center of the cross symbolizes God coming down to join with man. Jesus, the God-man the pefect go-between. The empty cross is the story of spirit incarnating in matter, then through Christ having the power to extricate itself.

DEATH — absence of life in the body, and/or the physical dissolution of the body. Death is caused by man's failure to comply fully with God's love.

It has been found quite possible, through the power of our thoughts and words, in affirming the opposite of life (or death) and talking or even thinking about death of our physical body in any form, our cells can be robbed of their natural life.

Let us not say "I am tired," "I am weak," or "I am sick;" but rather let us say, "I am strong," "I am well," "I am alive with the life of God now and forevermore to serve Him longer and better." I am aware this is VERY difficult and seemingly ridiculous in the presence of a splitting headache, extreme weariness, or anything serious. By all means, see your doctor, do all that you can to assist your body to heal itself, then try to 'accentuate the positive'.

The above procedure has been proven an amazing and scientific element in healing as recorded by medical doctors in RECOMMENDED READING at the end of this GLOSSARY.

DHARMA (dhar'-ma) — Sanskrit for law, especially the order, or law, of the universe. Dharma is action — Karma is reaction. Action once performed, the reaction is inevitable UNLESS prayer and/or grace has intervened. An individual has control over his actions. (See **KARMA**.)

ENLIGHTEN — to give the light of knowledge, to become free from ignorance, prejudice, or superstition; to inform; to give clarification as to meanings, intentions. ENLIGHT—ENMENT is becoming aware that there is more to know, to learn, to see and to hear. Especially in our context, pertaining to Spiritual Truths. ONE IS NEVER FULLY ENLIGHTENED while living on this Earth, except, of course, for Jesus, the Christ. However, enlightenment can come gradually through experiencing and learning . . . or in an instant.

ENTITY (en'-ti-ty) — the invisible being (with the soul) that exists after the human body ceases to function. ENTITIES plural.

ERROR — transgression; wrongdoing; the state of believing what is untrue or incorrect as true and right. Thinking or acting upon that which we know to be false or faulty. May be consciously done (sin) or unknowlingly (error). (See **SIN**.)

EVOLUTION (ev-o-lu'-tion) — the act or process of unfolding; development or growth, usually in slow stages and from simpler forms to those that are more complex . . . also, enlargement of the understanding of the conscious mind through intellectual pursuits; expanding our concepts higher and higher, i.e., We have 'evolved' materially from the use of candles, to oil lamps, to gas lights, to electric lighting.

Spiritually we evolve from thinking of God as an old man with white hair that sits on a throne in 'heaven' watching everything we do in case we need to be punished . . . to realizing that Jesus, the Christ, came to give us the greatest commandments. God has now become a loving, caring, Heavenly Father, whose greatest desire is to bring us, His children, made in His image and likeness, back to Him.

ESOTERIC (es-o-ter'-ic) — information (especially in the spiritual realm) taught to only a select number because the information could not be understood nor comprehended by the general population. Undoubtedly much of the teachings that Jesus taught His disciples when they were alone were of an esoteric nature. The Bible tells us that much of what Jesus told His disciples could not be comprehended by them at that time, but through later events much of His teachings began to make sense when they put into practice what they had learned as they 'evolved' or developed their spiritual understanding.

There is a beautiful ancient saying, *"When the pupil is ready, the teacher is there."*

FALSE PROPHET — deceptive thoughts that have been built up by error; selfish desires; self-delusion. They seem innocent and as harmless as lambs, but are in reality selfish and dangerous. *"Beware of false prophets, which come to you in sheep's clothing, but inwardly they are ravening wolves."* (Matthew 7:15)

GUARDIAN ANGEL — a special protector and guide that God gives to each soul at their physical birth.

GUIDE — a higher evolved, loving spirit who, having gone through many of the lessons that we have come to Earth to learn, has volunteered to be with us providing understanding, comfort, and guidance — especially to those souls who are already on a spiritual path. This entity has been with us from birth.

GURU (goo'-roo) — **SANSKRIT** word for spiritual teacher. This could be a special person who has spiritually influenced our lives by their particular interpretation of Truth, i.e., Dwight L. Moody, Dr. Harry A. Ironside, John Wesley, Martin Luther, etc. (See **HIGHER SELF**.)

HEAVEN — the space surrounding the earth created by God (Genesis 1:1). Also referred to as plural, heavens (Genesis 2:1). Mention is made in II Corinthians 12:2b of "*. . . one caught* ***up to the third heaven***." When one allows oneself to grow in a state of consciousness in harmony with the thoughts of God there is more and more a feeling of 'heaven on earth'.

HELL — let us think for a moment, spiritually, in the light of all we have talked about so far and approach hell in this manner.

When error or sin has reached its limit, the retroactive law asserts itself; and judgment, being a part of that law, brings its penalty upon the transgressor. This penalty is not punishment, but discipline, as difficult as it may seem to be at the time. When the transgressor repents and becomes obedient, he is forgiven.

Hell is symbolized by the purifying fire which consumes the dross of man's character. Time and space prohibits further teaching on this very Evangelical teaching, and would be a book in itself. Please remember, however, *"But, beloved, be not ignorant of this one thing, that one day is with the Lord as a thousand years, and a thousand years as one day. The Lord is not slack concerning his promise, as some men count slackness; but is longsuffering to us-ward, not willing that any should perish, but that all should come to repentence." (II Peter 3:8, 9)*

HIERARCHY (higher'-ar-key) — a ranking, so to speak, of individualized beings, including the **ARCHANGELS**, **ANGELS**, **SERAPHIM**, and **CHERUBIM**. A deeper physical meaning could be those higher evolved souls (entities) such as Master Teachers, adepts, sages, chelas, and other souls who are fulfilling and assisting us to fulfill God's ultimate plan for His highest creation.

In the Biblical connotation, we could consider the Master Jesus, his chosen 12 disciples, the 120 who met in the upper room for the baptism of the Holy Spirit, etc., as now representing the Hierarchy.

HIGHER SELF — the true inner self, the total of the soul's experience thus far. The part of the self which reincarnates, taking on different personalities to fit the life necessary to learn at that time, yet continuing to exist as a fragment from which the Higher Self is constructed . . . also known as the Christ Consciousness . . . or the Holy Spirit within us, especially after one has been 'born again' or truly decides they want to be on a spiritual path; the part of us that lovingly, continually reminds us of the lessons we have come to Earth to learn. Perhaps another name for the Higher Self would be our **CON—SCIENCE**.

When we ask or pray in Jesus' name, it is with a great desire for that consciousness which Jesus possessed; that in reality we are perfect children of the Father. If we would have God manifest through us, we must endeavor to raise our thoughts and feelings to the standard of God by the power of the Holy Spirit in the name of Jesus.

HOLISTIC or **WHOLISTIC** — that which pertains to the total being; recognizing, accepting, and working with the entire being — mentally, physically, emotionally, and spiritually. Usually applied to health and healing techniques, because all the above contributes to the health of an individual.

HOLY SPIRIT or **HOLY GHOST** — The Spirit is the infinite 'breath' of God, the life essence of Being. *"And when he had said this, he breathed on them, and saith unto them, Receive ye the Holy Spirit."* (John 20:22)

The Holy Spirit is the love of God taking care of the human family (family in the broad sense). The Holy Spirit is in the world today with great power and wisdom (since in reality, the Holy Spirit IS God). He is ready and desirous to be used and called upon for guidance and teaching, because His particular purpose is to teach and comfort; to bring all men into communion with God through the Christ. He is the one Jesus prophesied would come after He (Jesus) left, as recorded in the beautiful passage in John 14:16, 17. And then fulfilled in Acts 1 and 2.

To be 'filled with the Holy Spirit' is the realization of the activities of Spirit in the individual consciousness. This quickening is peculiar to each individual and must be experienced to be fully understood.

The Holy Spirit is the only authority that Jesus ever recognized as the one and only custodian of the true gospel and doctrine of God. This gospel (good news) should not come secondhand, but each must receive it for themselves from the Holy Spirit, sent by the Father (God) in the name of Jesus, the Christ, the Son, our way-show-er, and the 'first-fruits'. (See **JESUS**.)

The Holy Spirit is the true teacher of all Spiritual Truths. *"But the Comforter, which is the Holy Spirit, whom the Father will send in my name, he shall teach you all things, and bring all things to your remembrance, whatsoever I have said unto you."*. (John 14:26)

IDOL — any object of ardent or excessive devotion or admiration — scripturally means, a false god. Even as Jesus was tempted by Satan, we are also often tempted to worship the false gods of greed, revenge, jealousy, covetousness, and other forms of negative actions by our devotion and admiration. (See Galatians 5:19-21)

JESUS — The perfect expression of the Divine idea — man. Jesus' prayers were answered because He continually dwelt in perfect harmony with the Father (God). Christ is the perfect idea of God for man. The union of these two words, Jesus and Christ, is the idea and expression, of the perfect man demonstrated. Jesus is the human name of Christ and is the WAY—SHOW—ER. *"Jesus saith unto him, (Thomas) I am the way, the truth, and the life: no man cometh unto the Father, but by me."* (John 14:6) *". . . I am come that they might have life, and that they might have it more abundantly."* (John 10:10b) To awaken man to the possibilities of his own nature; *"As he (Jesus) is, so are we in this world."* (I John 4:17)

Jesus was fully conscious of God's character and His own relationship to Him. He knew God as unlimited love and as ever-present, abundant life, wisdom, and supply. A Father who is ready and willing to provide every need of the human heart. As the Son of God, Jesus had access to all that God is. Jesus didn't just believe that His words were true, He KNEW they were true! Vital, living words, which carried conviction and which produced immediate results.

He set into motion spiritual ideas that have been operating in the world ever since — a true representative of a thoroughly organized plan to help men into a higher realization of God and their relationship with Him.

"Jesus answered them, and said, My doctrine is not mine, but his that sent me." (John 7:16)

JUDGMENT — a mental act of evaluation through comparison or contrast thus coming to a decision. We are admonished to be very cautious not to judge others, their motives, or even their actions. *"Judge not, that ye be not judged. For with what judgment ye judge, ye shall be judged: and with what measure ye mete, it shall be measured to you again."* (Matthew 7:1-2)

Judgment belongs to God alone as many scriptures tell us. However, we are reminded to have spiritual discernment; the inner voice through whose expression we come into a larger realization of ourselves and others.

Judgment is a faculty of the mind that is exercised in

two ways — from (1) sense or intellectual perspective, or (2) spiritual understanding.

KARMA (car'-ma) — Sanskrit word meaning the effect of any act, religious or otherwise; the law of cause and effect regulating one's future life; inevitable retribution. To the Evangelical, it can be related to *"Be not deceived; God is not mocked: for whatsoever a man soweth, that shall he also reap."* (Galatians 6:7) Also, *"And let us not be weary in well doing: for in due-season we shall reap. . ."*. (Galatians 6:9)

Please keep in mind that this includes good deeds as well as those not so good. We reap what we sow . . . in the physical, very elementary sense, corn for corn, wheat for wheat, etc. This carries through in the material, emotional, mental, and spiritual sense.

KARMIC BOARD — a group of 25 very highly developed (evolved) entities before whom the soul appears at the proper time after the laying aside of the physical body. (Revelation 4:2-4) Their purpose is NOT to judge, YOU judge yourself. Their purpose is to lovingly guide, assist, advise and aid the soul to make decisions as to what to do next — and they have a special function in respect to the soul's next incarnation. God's Assistants, so to speak.

The 'Book of Life' or the Akasha is revealed in an 'instant' to them so they can perform their task wisely — where basically your memory is concerned, at that time, with what you were to achieve and whether you accomplished it in your most recent lifetime.

KNOWLEDGE — acquaintance with facts; range of information, awareness or understanding; enlightenment (*Webster*). Intellectual knowledge is independent of feeling; literal knowledge without consideration of the Spirit.

Man can store up a great amount of knowledge obtained from books and teachers, but the most unlettered man who sits at the feet of his Lord in silence comes forth radiant with the true knowledge — that of Spirit.

LAW — rules of conduct established and enforced by an authority. The Laws of God are just, exact, and undeviating as are the laws of mathematics. Law is a faculty of the mind, placing first things first. To recognize this is the starting point in finding God. Man does not make the spiritual laws, for they were established before the world was formed.

MEDIUM — an intermediate or intervening person through whom a force or energy acts. Many times the medium will actually turn their body or vocal cords over to a higher entity through which a message may be given in far more depth than the abilities of the one acting as the medium. Many true mediums consider this a positive and direct way of receiving deeper Truths since the Higher Entity does not go through the reasoning mind of the medium, who might feel the message is so unusual as not to be valid.

Could this be a reason why some of the prophets and/or disciples spoke 'in trance' (Acts 10:10-16; Acts 11:5-10; Acts 22:17-21) *". . . or whether in the body, or out of the body, I cannot tell: God knoweth."* (II Corinthians 12:2b)

What the prophets and/or disciples had to say or write was so completely out of the realm of their understanding that it was necessary for them to be an intermediary to receive the messages accurately. (See **TRANCE**)

Unfortunately, this facility has been misused, and some mediums have allowed their bodies, voices, hands, etc., to be taken over and used by 'less evolved' forces or entities. (See **CHANNEL**.)

METAPHYSICAL — (Author's note: I believe this one of the most misinterpreted and least understood words among the Evangelicals at this present time; and yet it is so simple.)

The dictionary says 'meta — after, beyond, higher ...' plus the word physical. Together the words means beyond or higher than what is readily apparent.

The Bible is one of the most metaphysical books ever written!

May I refer you to the INTRODUCTION PART I, where it is indicated that the Bible was written on at least three different levels, for the understanding of those newly converted, to the levels required by deeper seekers. ("When the pupil is ready, the teacher is there!")

Jesus' parables alone, while seemingly were just simple stories, have a depth of meaning that is inexhaustible. Jesus said in Matthew 13:13, *"Therefore speak I to them in parables: because they seeing see not; and hearing they hear not, neither do they understand."*

Let us continue with several parables in the 13th Chapter of Matthew. Jesus very clearly indicated that the original parable was given to and for the multitude, but the scripture also says that he gave a deeper meaning to the parables. The disciples began to ask Him as recorded in Matthew 13:36b *"Declare unto us the parable of the tares of the field."* So He gave them deeper Truths.

God is OH, SO willing that His babes, children and mature ones continue to grow and learn more and more of His immeasurable Truths. BUT *"He (Jesus) did not many mighty works there because of their unbelief."* (Matthew 13:58)

The ten commandments (Exodus 20:3-17) would represent milk — Truths requiring no spiritual insight to understand. A series of do's and don't's that are very clear and concise as they are given (MILK); yet, when Jesus' was asked to give the greatest commandment in Matthew 22:36-40, *"Master, which is the great commandment in the law? Jesus said unto him, Thou shalt love the Lord thy God with all thy heart, and with all thy soul, and with all thy mind. This is the first and great commandment. And the second is like unto it, Thou shalt love thy neighbour as thyself. On these two commandments hang all the law and the prophets."*

In studying, we find that the first four of the ten commandments ARE contained in the greatest commandment *"Thou shalt love the Lord thy God with all thy heart, and with all thy soul, and with all thy mind."* (Matthew 22:37b), the next six of the ten commandments are contained in Jesus' statement *". . . second is like unto it, Thou shalt love thy neighbour as thyself."* (Matthew 22:39) The ability to condense the ten commandments into two is MEAT!

You see, there is a time to understand and a time to just trust and have faith. *"These things understood not his disciples at the first: BUT when Jesus was glorified, then remembered they that these things were written of him, and that they had done these things unto him."* (John 12:16)

John 16:4 *"But these things have I told you, that when the time shall come, you may remember that I told you of them. And these things I said not unto you at the beginning, because I was with you."* Was the time not right?

My very favorite verse regarding this subject is John 16:12, 13 *"I have yet many things to say unto you, but ye cannot bear them now. Howbeit when he, the Spirit of Truth, is come, he will guide you unto ALL truth: for he shall not speak of himself; but whatsoever he shall hear, that shall he speak: and he will shew you things to come."*

I encourage you to not take negatively some of these beautiful words simply because the adversary has chosen to have them so misinterpreted and misunderstood that we lose the opportunity to grow to the 'beyond' and 'higher' SPIRITUAL TRUTH!

METAPHYSICS (met'a-phys'-ics) — a way of life through the Holy Spirit, who helps you to live your life 'more abundantly' (See John 10:10) by controlling your thoughts, words, actions, emotions, and deeds.

METAPHYSICIAN — one who sincerely seeks to live beyond the physical by controlling their thoughts, words, actions, emotions and deeds, through the power of the Holy Spirit.

We CAN and DO create our own life and circumstances to a great extent.

First comes the THOUGHT, then the WORD, strengthened by EMOTION, and that combination shapes our life; i.e., someone thinks because they are sitting in a drafty area they will get a chill and 'catch a cold'. They mention to a friend close by that this is so — strengthening their emotional response; sure enough, they have said it and soon they have what they declared they would have . . . a cold.

Certainly we realize that we should do all in our power to take care of this body-temple that God has provided us, but if you find yourself in a situation as stated above, say to yourself AND AT LEAST ONE OTHER PERSON, with a strong emotional feeling, "I'm catching more health from this air that I am receiving so abundantly." It works!

One other example, and this **has** worked for myself as well as others. When a 'lump' or growth of any kind appears in or on your body, the temple of the Holy Spirit, repeat with emotion and conviction "Every plant which my Heavenly Father has not planted shall be rooted up. God's love in me is a consuming fire, utterly destroying you, because God did not make you, and it is not His will that you find a place in my system. I ask in Jesus' name that anything in me nourishing a false growth be removed. All error is now dissolved from my consciousness through Divine Love, and I am saturated with harmony, order, and wholeness of Spirit."** Say this as you direct your thought toward a particular growth, as many times as you think of it . . . and then be delightfully suprised.

**Taken loosely from a portion of *DIVINE REMEDIES*

compiled by Theodosia DeWitt Schobert and published by Unity Books, Lee's Summit, MO. (Now out of print.)

MILLENIUM (mil-len'-nee-um) — a period of one thousand years during which the Christ will reign on Earth . . . a period of great happiness, peace, prosperity, etc. As spoken of in Revelation and believed by Evangelicals, but not actually mentioned as such in the Bible.

MYSTIC (mis'tic) — the acquisition of power for the Glory of God. One who professes to have mystical experiences by which he intuitively comprehends Truths beyond human understanding. A true spiritual mystic never forgets when asked as in John 10:24b, 25 *"If thou be the Christ, tell us plainly. Jesus answered them, I told you, and ye believed not: the works that I do in my Father's name, they bear witness of me."*

NEOPHYTE (ne'-o-fite) — a new convert, a beginner, or novice.

NEW BIRTH — the glorious awakening of man to a consciousness of unity with the one universal Spirit; changing from mortal to spiritual consciousness through the quickening power of the Word of Truth. (See **BORN AGAIN** and **CONVERSION**.)

OCCULT (oc-cult) — (Author's note: I feel this is another of those words that is misinterpreted and misunderstood) for it simply means, that which is hidden, beyond ordinary human understanding; mysterious. The full-of-wonder (wonderful) teaching of the Triune God is an occult teaching, since it was 'hidden' for centuries to the Old Testament individuals and is difficult for the mind to comprehend the love of God for us, His ultimate creation. The teaching of the millenium and the rapture were also 'hidden' until it was time for the teaching to be revealed.

Sad to say, the adversary again has clouded this word with negative misconceptions. We associate the occult with black magic, Satanic worship, voodoo, and all the

the extreme negative aspects of that which we do not understand instead of realizing that the meaning is simply a completely hidden Truth . . . until the right time to be revealed.

Perhaps it is difficult for you to accept and change your thinking but do consider the real teaching, and may I reiterate the suggestion that you do not allow the adversary to rob you of ALL TRUTH!

OCCULTISM — the desire to search out and learn as much about these 'hidden' teachings, seemingly incomprehensible Truths. In a negative sense, the acquisition and laws of the universe for personal gain and power. A law is a law — and will work regardless of the intention of the mind behind it; i.e., the law of gravity is truly wonderful — but in the wrong hands or the wrong mind behind it, it could be used to push a heavy stone from a cliff onto an individual. (See **PSYCHIC**.)

PISCEAN AGE (pi-see'-an) — that period of approximately 2000 years during which time Christianity has been practiced. Pisces, astrologically, is the sign of the fish, and several of Jesus' disciples were fishermen. In the days of early church, the fish was the sign a Christian would give another to secretly admit they were followers of Christ's teachings. Time and space in this book prevents our discussing the approximately 2000 year period during which God dealt with His human creation in specific ways (these periods are known to the Evangelical as Dispensations). Therefore, let us just say that the Piscean Age is at an end, and we are now in the **AQUARIAN AGE** when Christ's teachings will dominate and manifest more and more.

PRAYER — communication from man to God; taking place in the innermost part of man's being. Prayer can accelerate mental action to synchronize it with the Higher Self or the Christ Mind. It is the particular language of spirituality. It is not just 'asking', but praising and affirming

Truths that exist.

By complying with God's laws, through prayer, we can truly *"Seek ye first the kingdom of God and His righteousness; and all these things shall be added unto you."* (Matthew 6:33)

Jesus, himself, felt it necessary and important to pray; even teaching His disciples to do so. (Matthew 6:9-13)

"Rejoice evermore. Pray without ceasing. In everything give thanks: for this is the will of God in Christ Jesus concerning you." (I Thessalonians 5:16-18 and to the end of the chapter)

It is important that when we pray to have faith believing that we shall receive. (Mark 9:23; Mark 11:22, 23; and many, many others.)

PSYCHIC (sigh'-keek) — of the psyche, or mind, beyond natural or known physical processes — sensitive to forces beyond the physical world. Just as we now realize that our mind is indeed a mighty force — thus we have the study of psychology and treatment of neuroses, emotions, and repressions through psychoanalysis.

Also, anything not seen or understood by intellectual or conscious reasoning. A person who is sensitive to this force (or forces) is called a psychic. One having mental powers not common to ordinary man, but not yet quickened to the standard of the Holy Spirit.

RAPTURE, THE (rap'- shure) — a belief by most Evangelicals as a time when Jesus Christ will come back, recognizable, as prophecied *"And when he had spoken these things, while they beheld, he was taken up; and a cloud received him out of their sight. And while they looked stedfastly toward heaven as he went up, behold, two men stood by them in white apparel; Which also said, Ye men of Galilee, why stand ye gazing up into heaven? this same Jesus, which is taken up from you into heaven, shall so come in like manner as ye have seen him go into* *heaven."* (Acts 1:9-11)

Also *"For the Lord himself shall descend from heaven with a shout, with the voice of the archangel, and with the trump of God: and the dead in Christ shall rise first: Then we which are alive and remain shall be caught up together with them in the clouds, to meet the Lord in the air: and so shall we ever be with the Lord."* (I Thessalonians 4:16, 17)

It is assumed to be alluded to in the passage *"Then shall two be in the field; the one shall be taken, and the other left. Two women shall be grinding at the mill; the one shall be taken, and the other left. Watch therefore: for ye know not what hour your Lord doth come."* (Matthew 24:40-42)

Perhaps it should be noted here that in the verses preceeding (Matthew 24:36-39), Matthew is speaking about the days of Noah and likens it to the time mentioned above — in verse 39 *"...and took them all away..."* — *yet* Noah and his family (the righteous — eight in all) were left.

Those that may expect to 'meet the Lord in the air' are those Evangelicals who look for His coming and are like the 'wise virgins' who prepared for the coming of the bridegroom and had 'oil' in their lamps (Matthew 25:1-13). The 'foolish' virgins did not prepare for the bridegroom, had not been converted/born-again and supposedly will remain here on earth to go through the TRIBULATION (as taught by the Evangelicals who teach regarding the RAPTURE).

Please read the beautiful prayer of Jesus to God, just previous to His betrayal (John 17) in its entirety, especially noting where Jesus prays *"I pray not that thou shouldest take them out of the world, but that thou shouldest keep them from evil. They are not of the world, even as I am not of the world. Sanctify them through thy truth: thy word is truth."* (John 17:15-17)

REINCARNATION (re-in-car-na'-tion) — rebirth of the soul into another human body. Reincarnation will continue until the ego awakens to the Christ Spirit and begins its journey back to the Father, finally attaining that of which Jesus spoke in John 17.

REGRESSION (re-gresh'-ion) — a journey of the soul mentally 'back in time' to another time, place and/or situation assisting the evolving individual to be reminded of that which they came to do in this lifetime. Sometimes this occurs in dreams, in moments of meditation or contemplation; or can be done through self-hypnosis, hypnosis, or any altered state of consciousness.

(There is also the opposite, PROGRESSION, when through the above practices one can be made aware of some future event.)

RELIGION — any specific system of belief, worship, etc., often involving a code of ethics; a state of mind or way of life expressing love for and trust in God or an object of conscientious pursuit.

We should keep in mind the three activities of consciousness: spiritual, psychical, and physical. In a synoptic review, the spiritual is the realm of absolute principles; the psychical, or astral, is the realm of thought images; and the physical is the realm of manifestation.

Jesus, the type of well-balanced, thoroughly developed man, comprehends and consciously adjusts His spirit, soul, and body as a whole. Those individuals on the way to this attainment have various experiences, symbolically set forth in the Scriptures.

REPENTANCE (re-pent'-ance) — a feeling of sorrow or remorse for wrongdoing. Turning away from sin/error to a true belief in God and righteousness; a reversal of mind and heart into the direction of that which is of God . . . a breaking with mortal thought and ascending into a spiritual thought realm, the kingdom of God. (See **BORN AGAIN** and **CONVERSION**.)

SAGE — a wise and perceptive person, known for his wisdom, experience, and good judgment. (See **WISDOM**.)

SALVATION (sal-va'-tion) — restoration of man to his spiritual birthright; regaining conscious possession of his God-given attributes. It is a free gift of God to man, and embodies a knowledge of God that frees one from all limitations and points the way which mind and body may be lifted up in spiritual consciousness.

Just the belief that Jesus, in a physical way, atoned for our sins is not salvation because salvation is an inner overcoming, a change of consciousness; a cleansing of the mind, through Christ, from thoughts of evil/sin/error.

SANCTIFICATION (sanc'-ti-fi-ca'-tion) — completely covering oneself with the nature of God, thus rising to the plane of dominion that gives man peace and satisfaction; knowing the purity and holiness of the Christ consciousness. *"This is the will of God, even your sanctification ..."* (I Thessalonians 4:3a) *"Sanctify them through thy truth: thy word is truth."* (John 17:17)

SANSKRIT (san'scrit) — the classical Old Indic literary language: it has provided the chief clue in the charting of Indo-European languages.

SERAPHIM (ser'-a-fim) — a very high and noble order of angels.

SILVER CORD — a concentrated form of energy linking the physical body to the astral body and higher bodies. This is severed at the physical death of the mortal body, referred to in Ecclesiastes 12:6.

SIN — 'missing the mark', or falling short of Divine perfection. Sin is man's failure to express the fruit of the Spirit; love, joy, peace, longsuffering (patience), gentleness (kindness), goodness, faith, meekness (humility), and temperance (self-control) as recorded in Galatians 5:22, 23. Plus those other attributes of God that we had when we were created. Sin is first mental *"For as he* *thinketh in his heart, so is he:"* (Proverbs 23:7); *"The thought of foolishness is sin:"* (Proverbs 24:9a); *"Charity (love) . . . thinketh no evil."* (I Corinthians 13:4a, 5b); *"Whosoever hateth his brother is a murderer:"* (I John 3:15) We are encouraged to *"Be ye transformed by the renewing of your mind, that ye may prove what is that good, and acceptable, and perfect, will of God."* (Romans 12:2b) Also known as ERROR.

SOLAR PLEXUS — a large nerve center lying back of the pit of the stomach, controlling the activity of the stomach. It is the vital center of the organism through which the subconscious mind connects with the physical body, giving rise to the saying, "a gut feeling".

SOUL — the spiritual part of the person having the functions of thinking and willing. *"And the Lord God formed man of the dust of the ground, and breathed into his nostrils the breath of life; and man became a living soul."* (Genesis 2:7) That which God formed in His likeness and image (See Genesis 1:26, 27 and 5:1). Though fallen, man continually seeks to find his way back to God, his Creator . . . with full cooperation and longing desire from the Father.

The Soul includes the conscious and subconscious minds.

SPIRIT — the life principle in men, invisible, but of the higher body. *"God is a spirit: and they that worship him must worship him in spirit and in truth."* (John 4:24) Man is spirit, soul, and body. Spirit is the I AM, the individuality. The body is soul expressing. (See **SOUL**)

TABERNACLE — represents the physical temporary body of man, and the soul. It is when we are in the body that we are drawn by the Holy Spirit to a knowledge of the Christ and God. *"No man can come to me, except the Father which hath sent me draw him:"* (John 6:44) The tabernacle is a temporary dwelling place; however, *"Yea, I think it meet, as long as I am in this taberncle, to stir you* *up by putting you in rememberance; Knowing that shortly I must put off this my tabernacle . . .*" (II Peter 1:13, 14a) Truly this is the place where God meets us, or where we 'meet' God or become aware of need of the Christ and Holy Spirit. (See **TEMPLE**.)

TAROT (tare'-o) or (ta-ro') — there are about as many explanations to the Tarot cards' origin as there are cards (a collection of 78).

A pictorial Bible, or a pictorial journey of the soul, especially the Major Arcana, which are the first 22 cards. The Minor Arcana cards remaining are the lessons or challenges encountered, or to be encountered, as well as the possible positive attributes to assist the soul on its journey.

Regardless as to the country or date of origin, it is usually believed they originated during some time when it was forbidden to teach and extol the principles of God and Jesus, the Christ . . . or perhaps the people could not read or remember and thus the 'picture cards'. The people did know (or the word was passed around) the spiritual meaning of numbers, symbols, and colors. Slowly but surely these spiritual Truths were formed into pictorial cards and passed around from person to person, group to group.

When the Tarot is studied, or viewed in this way, it is outstanding — and unbelievably meaningful and beautiful. Everything on the card has an awesome significance, but because of the present way these wonderful cards have been misused, the adversary is again robbing the Evangelical of a powerful teaching tool.

Regardless of the 'deck' of cards used — they are remarkably similar in their interpretation, and are an excellent tool for teaching young children, babes in Christ or even maturing Christians.

Many have not studied their spiritual significance and use these marvelous cards as a method of 'fortune-telling'.

Please don't hold that against the Tarot. I have spoken with people who do the same with the Bible, but remember the saying "It's the exceptions that prove the rule."

The Tarot is not to be feared any more than God and/or the Holy Spirit is to be feared, but rather appreciated and respected for all that it contains.

We know Jesus taught in parables so the people could more readily understand . . . then why not parables in pictures?

TEMPLE — the more permanent dwelling place of the Holy Spirit, the Christ, God — or as the Bible says *"Know ye not that ye are the temple of God, and that the spirit of God dwelleth in you? If any man defile the temple of God, him shall God destroy; for the temple of God is holy, which temple ye are."* (I Corinthians 3:16, 17)

"What? know ye not that your body is the temple of the Holy Ghost (Spirit) which is in you, which ye have of God, and ye are not your own? For ye are bought with a price: therefore glorify God in your body, and in your spirit, which are God's." (I Corinthians 6:19, 20)

The Holy Spirit has revealed to me that the difference between the body/soul tabernacle and the body/soul temple is the temporary versus the permanent. Once a body/soul really becomes determined to live their life totally for Christ, perhaps through many incarnations, his/her body becomes an acknowledged permanent dwelling place for the Christ. As mature Christians, truly we should be more aware that the above verses are indeed true and we are not our own, the awareness of our responsibility for this body temple becomes so important and we begin to, i.e., eat to live, not live to eat — to take care of ourselves — not for ego, but because it is our privilege and duty as the 'Temple of the Holy Spirit' . . . where God dwells.

TRANCE — a state resembling sleep in which consciousness may or may not remain, as in hypnosis; a condition of great mental abstraction as that of a religious mystic or spiritual person in which the 'thinking' or 'evaluating' part of man is bypassed so that they are unable to reason, "This can't be happening to me" or "I can't be seeing or saying this".

The Bible speaks several times of this occurring to men of God, when God actually spoke to them such as Genesis 15:12, recorded as a deep sleep when God spoke to Abram; Numbers 24:4b when Balaam had the spirit of God come upon him and prophecied as he "*. . . saw the vision of the Almighty, falling into a trance, but having his eyes open:*" and in Acts 22:17 when Saul said that even while he prayed in the temple, he was in a trance.

In II Corinthians 12:2, 3, Paul remembered "*. . . a man in Christ above fourteen years ago, (whether in the body, I cannot tell; or whether out of the body, I cannot tell: God knoweth;) such an one caught up to the third heaven . . . caught up into paradise, and heard unspeakable words . . .*" (verse 4)

Peter, while food was preparing, "*. . . fell into a trance, and saw heaven opened . . .*" Acts 10:10b and Peter, himself, doubted what this vision should mean (verse 17).

Revelation 1:9, 10 when John, on the Isle of Patmos, was in the Spirit and received the Revelation.

TRANSMIGRATION (trans-my-gra'-tion) — the belief that the soul can or does go into another life form other than human after death, such as a plant, animal, insect, etc. This is not a belief held by most reincarnationists of whom I am acquainted. We do believe that God created man in His own image and likeness as mentioned many times previously; and that reincarnation is His loving, gracious, and glorious plan whereby we choose to return to that which He has desired for us from the very beginning.

TRIBULATION, THE — believed by many Evangelicals

to be a seven (7) year period following the RAPTURE when those who truly followed Jesus have gone to meet him in the clouds (Jesus is not expected to return to earth at that time) so those left behind have had some knowledge of what would happen at the RAPTURE and when it occurs, they immediately become 'believers'. It is supposedly during this time that Satan/Devil/the adversary is loosed with full power, because the prayers, influence, and strength of the Evangelicals has been removed by the RAPTURE. Then will come the full wrath of the adversary as recorded in the Book of Daniel (Old Testament) and The Revelation (New Testament).

This seven years is expected to be so horrible that it will have to be shortened, or no one would survive. Please read the entire chapter of Matthew 24, especially verses 21, 22. After the TRIBULATION, the Battle of Armageddon is expected. A battle in the Heavens between the 'armies' of Good and Evil. THEN after God has taken over again (because, of course, God, the Good, WILL win), Jesus, the Bridegroom, will return with His Bride (those who went with Him in the RAPTURE) to rule and reign for the 1000 years known as the MILLENIUM.

Many Evangelicals who believe that the RAPTURE will occur before the TRIBULATION are refered to as PRE-TRIBULATION BELIEVERS; those who believe that the RAPTURE will occur in the middle of the seven years (or after three and one half years — a very important number in this particular study) are called MID-TRIBULATION BELIEVERS, and those who believe the RAPTURE will take place after the TRIBULATION are called POST-TRIBULATION BELIEVERS.

This is a very brief explanation of these doctrines. If you feel it necessary to delve into further depth, there are many books and scholars who will be happy to assist you in obtaining additional information.

WHOLISTIC — have to do with the composite body, especially applied to health. Interrelation between the psychical, mental, and physical aspects. (Please see **HOLISTIC**.)

WISDOM — can be obtained through learning and intelligence; however, it is possible to be intelligent and have an abundance of knowledge, yet not be wise. But the wise man, or one who has wisdom, will possess intelligence and knowledge.

Also an intuitive knowing; listening to the voice of God within as the source of our understanding. Wisdom includes judgment, discrimination, intuition, and all the departments of mind that come under the head of knowing.

Please read Proverbs 3; 4; and 16 especially to understand the important credibility given to wisdom.

YOGA — a Sanskrit word meaning union; a practice involving complete concentration upon something, especially God, in order to establish union. HATHA YOGA is the practice of attempting to attain this union between the physical body and the mind/spirit of God. Deliberate movements are done with concentration for a purpose.

It is an excellent discipline, most helpful for exercise without strenuous physical strain as each 'posture' is done slowly and rhythmically ONLY until strain is felt. One comes to a greater appreciation of this wonderful body-temple God has given each individual. (See Recommended Reading at the end of this Book.)

RECOMMENDED READING

THE HOLY BIBLE — Authorized King James Version
(due to its universal acceptance)

WEBSTER'S NEW WORLD DICTIONARY (Concise Edition)
The World Publishing Company
Cleveland and New York (1962)

REINCARNATION IN CHRISTIANITY
by Dr. Geddes MacGregor
The Theosophical Publishing House
Wheaton, IL (Second Printing 1981)

BORN AGAIN AND AGAIN by John Van Auken
Inner Vision Publishing Company
1218 Eaglewood Drive
Virginia Beach, VA 23454 (1985)

LIFE BEFORE BIRTH — LIFE ON EARTH — LIFE AFTER DEATH by Paul E. Chu
Word View Press
Post Office Box 15
Fort Lee, NJ 07024 (Second Printing 1976)

REINCARNATION — ONE LIFE, MANY BIRTHS
by Rev. Noel Street
The Lotus Ashram, Inc.
Post Office Box 39
Fabens, TX 79838 (1978)

SOMEONE ASKED, HE ANSWERED
by Rev. Harold C. Curbin
CSA Press
Lakemont, GA (1970)

NONE OF THESE DISEASES by S. I. McMillen, D.D.
Fleming H. Revell Company
Old Tappan, NJ (Fifth Printing 1968)

THE REVEALING WORD by Charles Fillmore
Unity School of Christianity
Lee's Summit, MO (1959)

CHRISTIAN YOGA by J. M. Dechanet (a French Monk)
(1960 — now out of print)

YOGA IN TEN EASY LESSONS by J. M. Dechanet
Harper Row Publishers
New York, NY (English Edition 1965)

THE BIBLE AND THE TAROT by Corinne Heline
DeVorss Co., Publisher
Marina Del Ray, CA (1984)

JEWELS OF THE WISE by Epiphany Press
Epiphany Press
San Francisco, CA (1979)

WHO'S THE MATTER WITH ME? by Alice Steadman
DeVorss Company
Post Office Box 550
Marina Del Rey, CA 90294-0550 (Fifth Printing 1984)

LOVE, MEDICINE MIRACLES by Bernie S. Siegel, M.D.
Harper Row, Publishers
New York, NY (1986)

VIBRATIONAL MEDICINE by Richard Gerber, M.D.
Bear Company
Santa Fe, NM (1988)

ON DEATH AND DYING by Elizabeth Kubler-Ross, M.D.
MacMillan Publishing Co.
New York, NY 10022 (1969)

LIFE AFTER LIFE by Raymond A. Moody, Jr.
Bantam Books, Inc.
666 5th Ave., New York, NY 10103 (1975)

NOTES

NOTES

Dear Reader,

I pray this book has been a means of opening your mind & heart to deeper Spiritual Truths.

Many times I have been led to rewrite, revise, add to, & delve deeper into another line of thought by the Holy Spirit. Realizing this, please understand that I expect Him to continue working with me teaching more & more, deeper & deeper Truths; so what has been said at this point in time may continue to grow. I trust you have felt & will feel the same thing.

If you have had a death or near-death experience & would like to share it with me I would be delighted — just write me in care of the publisher.

Lovingingly,

Marilynn McDermott

In Appreciation

A note of appreciation to Haywood Press, Inc., of Waynesville, North Carolina. They were responsible for type selection, layout and typesetting.

Heartfelt thanks to Eugene Engdahl and his comprehensive Biblical knowledge in editing the manuscript and writing analysis prior to typesetting.

Their assistance made this book possible.

" . . . I think it is fantastic, it is so simply stated that even a beginner in metaphysics can understand it. The Bible quotes are so interesting and true. The Glossary is great. I wouldn't change a thing. You are holding a gem in this book."

Rev. Marnie Koski
Pastor, TV & Seminar Teacher

"Today, as there has been for thousands of years, there is a sad deficit of the ability to love and understand one another. We see more of the diversities of life rather than the unity that exists between countries and people . . . politics, education and, sadly between religious beliefs.

"Perhaps the most difficult gulf of all to overcome has been the increasing distance between our brethren who follow the Evangelical path of Christianity and those who follow the Metaphysical path, coming from diverse religious and philosophical backgrounds. In her book *Reincarnation - A Biblical Doctrine?,* Dr. McDirmit poses numerous fine examples of Biblical references that point the way to closing this gap between Evangelical and Metaphysical philosophies. This is not only a deeply referenced work, but tremendously readable. Directed towards the enlightened Mystical Christian who is searching for the answer to the question of whether they can still remain loyal to their beliefs as well as embrace the ancient Truth Teaching of the Reincarnated Soul, Dr. McDirmit does a splendid job in becoming a BRIDGE to span the gulf of misunderstanding. To read this book is to really begin to widen your personal doorway to the Mystical Christ dwelling within you . . . a Christed Presence that has followed you successively, through the far remembrances of past lives."

Roberta S. Herzog, D.D.
Lecturer, Author, Seminar Truth Teacher